Dear Bride-to-be,

Whether you have a large formal wedding or an intimate informal celebration, you need guidance in the logistics of putting together a personally memorable wedding and reception. As fashion editor of Modern Bride, *Jacqueline McCord Leo has spent many years selecting and styling beautiful wedding fashions for every type of bride. Combining this experience with personal interviews and extensive research, Mrs. Leo gives us a book filled with innovative ideas and up-to-date information that answer questions today's couples face. Budget is a major concern in the 1980s, which leads Mrs. Leo to advise alternative ways to share expenses. If yours is a second wedding, we have tips for you, too. Times* have *changed and THE NEW WOMAN'S GUIDE TO GETTING MARRIED reflects these changes. We are very proud that a member of our staff has so competently addressed herself to this need in contemporary life. There is no better guide to wedding planning in the eighties.*

Cele Goldsmith Lalli
Editor
Modern Bride

The New Woman's Guide to Getting Married

Jacqueline McCord Leo

BANTAM BOOKS
TORONTO · NEW YORK · LONDON · SYDNEY

THE NEW WOMAN'S GUIDE TO GETTING MARRIED
A Bantam Book / March 1982

PRINTING HISTORY
Marriage Information Chart reprinted courtesy World Almanac and Book of Facts 1982 Edition © 1981 by Newspaper Enterprise Association, Inc., 200 Park Avenue, New York, N.Y. 10166.

Cover photograph by Micheal Reinhardt.

Book designed by Renée Gelman.

Library of Congress Cataloging in Publication Data

Leo, Jacqueline McCord.
The new woman's guide to getting married.
1. Weddings. 2. Finance, Personal. I. Title.
HQ745.M35 395'.22 81-17548
ISBN 0-553-01375-0 (pbk.) AACR2

Published simultaneously in the United States and Canada

Bantam Books are published by Bantam Books, Inc. Its trademark, consisting of the words "Bantam Books" and the portrayal of a rooster, is Registered in U.S. Patent and Trademark Office and in other countries. Marca Registrada. Bantam Books, Inc., 666 Fifth Avenue, New York, New York 10103.

PRINTED IN THE UNITED STATES OF AMERICA

0 9 8 7 6 5 4 3 2

for John

Contents

Preface

After helping a number of friends with their weddings during the last few years, I began to recognize the obvious: most people want to marry. Though marriage was maligned for at least a decade and divorce rates soared, the desire to make that march down the aisle actually increased. Almost twenty-four million weddings are projected for the 1980s.

But today's wedding is not always the final chapter in a storybook romance—not when over 30 percent of all marriages are remarriages. And today's couple has little time in their busy schedules to plan a wedding and reception that once might have taken a year or more to organize. More changes: ten years ago, the bride's median age was twenty-one; today it is twenty-five. And with this maturity comes a different approach to weddings—more savvy and sophisticated than ever before. Today's couple earns two incomes, shares responsibilities equally, waits until both partners have established careers before contemplating having children, and lives and works where financial opportunities exist (often far from parents and families). And when they marry, whether traditionally or nontraditionally, they want clear-cut, down-to-earth advice about how to plan a wedding.

The New Woman's Guide to Getting Married is a comprehensive contemporary book that covers every conceivable kind of wedding—from a small private affair to a glittering ceremony and reception for hundreds. I've integrated second weddings throughout the book, since social taboos about divorced people remarrying no longer exist. Also, costs for goods and services are based on current prices and will certainly rise with inflation.

It became clear early on that couples also want new information on money and the law, how to merge possessions, and especially, how to cope with planning a wedding. All of this research has been incorporated to serve the contemporary bride and groom.

I would like to thank *Modern Bride* magazine and Bantam Books for their guidance and support, especially my editors, Linda Cunningham and Maxine Bartow. Also, a special thank-you to my researchers, Viola Jasous and Lisa Napoli—and to my husband, John Leo, for putting up with it all.

—Jackie McCord Leo

The New Woman's Guide to Getting Married

1 · Your Wedding—Trauma or Triumph?

A respectful hush fell over the crowd as the music started, and all eyes turned toward the center aisle. One by one the bridesmaids appeared, their concentration fixed on making their feet obey the unnatural rhythm of the wedding march. Someone reminded them to smile, and the first blinding flash sparked a series of clicks and lights that made it even harder to assemble gracefully at the altar. As if rehearsed, the guests began to murmur and coo as the bride started her long walk. "Isn't she beautiful," one said, answering her own question.

Few noticed that the woman in white was leaning on her father rather than being escorted by him. Or that the long, lacy dress looked as though it were a size too large. Or that she seemed to be shaking from the cold on that hot August day. And when she swooned for a few seconds at the altar, everyone thought, All brides are nervous—it's perfectly natural. The guests remembered it as a lovely traditional wedding, but the bride looks back on the whole experience as a nightmare.

Whether you call it premarital tension, wedding jitters, or engagement stress, nuptialphobia—fear of the wedding—can be as much a part of getting married as having a blood test. It starts almost as soon as you decide to marry. You think about that good friend who battled her way to the altar trying to salvage her plans against the wishes of others, and you're thrown into a psychological tailspin that increases your therapy from two to five sessions a week. The reasons for the trauma often have nothing to do with the idea of making a lifelong commitment to another person; what throws people is the idea of planning a wedding and going through what some women describe as the ultimate sorority hazing.

Nuptialphobia is characterized by the following symptoms: (1) Breaking out in a cold sweat each time you call your mother, (2) getting a headache each time his mother calls to tell you about another ideal caterer, (3) developing an allergic reaction to cold shrimp and hot roast beef, (4) getting writer's cramp from addressing too many invitations, and (5) having an uncontrollable desire to scream at and punch your future spouse.

Now it's true that nuptialphobia doesn't strike every bride. If you elope, you'll avoid this syndrome altogether, but you'll probably suffer some postwedding guilt about not sharing the occasion with the family that nurtured you as a child and the friends who supported you as an adult. If you leave it all up to your mother, you won't get nervous, but you also won't feel it's your wedding. And if you pay a wedding consultant to do it all for you, you may ease the tension but wind up starring in an independently produced off-Broadway production that has nothing to do with your life.

If you think nuptialphobia is a phenomenon that grew out of our complicated postwar society, you're wrong. Back in 1935, a book called *Weddings without Worry* was dedicated to "every engaged couple in the hope that it may save them much of the distracting anxiety which we ourselves experienced in preparing for that great event." And the authors, M. and S. Bee, cautioned their readers as follows: "So at this important period, let both parties [bride and groom] make ample allowances for nervous outbreaks and sentimental eccentricities."

Even my mother, who was married in that same year, remembers battling the family czars to have her wedding her way. Her first instinct was to avoid the grand reception, where, as she put it, "the clan would gather to criticize the food, the music, and the hosts." Having won that round, she proceeded to turn down a wealthy aunt's offer to provide an elaborate wedding dress. Mother never did like the idea of spending a fortune on a dress she would wear once, so she bought her entire outfit (a silk shantung suit, straw picture hat, and peau de soie shoes) on sale at Best & Company.

Having alienated her aunt and the rest of the family, she had only to deal with my grandmother, who, in the true ethnic tradition, allowed a group of women mourners into the house on the day of the wedding. Their job—to cry for my mother's impending loss of virginity. My mother, it seems, wasn't buying any of it, so she calmly explained, "Either they go, or I call off the wedding."

Today mother admits that a rebellious attitude is no way to run a wedding. The best way to neutralize your fears and plan your wedding with style and efficiency is to understand the problems you'll be facing, the decisions you'll have to make, and most important—what you want your wedding to be.

It's probable that the last time you and your parents collaborated on a party was the occasion of your eighth birthday. It didn't matter much that your cousin Lisa had to be invited and that your mother didn't let your sleep-over turn into an all-night giggle session. Back then, your parents' ideas prevailed to serve the family's best interests. Now that you're getting married, you might want your parents involved, but on your terms. The trick is to keep their interest without giving up control.

One way to do this is to make it clear that you need their advice and that you intend to consult with them often, even though you'll be making the decisions. Still, it's not exactly natural to plan a social event with your parents. You might have spent years developing a life away from them. It's not that you don't love and admire your family, but part of growing up is having your own friends and social identity.

One mother explained, "We don't have to win—we just want to be listened to with the same respect that our children give their friends." Fair enough. But one bride put it this way: "I knew I was in trouble when my mother thought that fish in aspic was a tuna casserole with Jell-O for dessert, not worthy of a proper wedding buffet."

Her parents had given her every opportunity to have a life outside of their working-class community, but an education and a big-city career only widened the social gap. "I was lucky," she explained. "My parents simply decided to tolerate and accept my fancy ideas. And once they did, I found myself wanting to simplify the whole affair."

For young brides, the wedding is often balanced in favor of their past, not their future. If the couple is not socially established, the wedding will honor the family rather than the friends, but for the growing number of women marrying for the first time between the ages of twenty-five and thirty, as well as the 720,000 people each year marrying again, the wedding is apt to be the kind of celebration that involves their friends rather than their long-lost cousins; their business associates rather than their fathers' golf partners; and their idea of party giving rather than that of their mothers.

"A wedding can be the first adult statement that a couple makes about themselves," says psychologist Eric Margenau. "It describes how the couple will relate socially in the future. If the wedding is predominantly for the family, it can mean that the family's needs and the couple's relationship to the family are significant, or that the couple doesn't have the strength of character to say, 'It's our wedding; we'd like it this way!'"

The problem is that a lot of brides start to feel guilty about denying their parents' wishes and cave in after a certain amount of resistance. Dr. Margenau advises the bride to "accept the guilt and go ahead with her own plans. It can be a healthy, maturing experience, and it shouldn't be avoided. It can prepare her for future life decisions and their accompanying anxiety—most of which she will make independently from her mother."

Still, nobody wants a battle royal over whether the stuffed mushrooms should be hot or cold, and no one's identity should be threatened if the band plays "Fascination." It all comes down to the adult art of communication and compromise—as much a part of a good wedding as a tear-jerking ceremony.

When Maggie and Tom became engaged in their senior year of college, they thought of having a small church wedding and inviting close family and friends. "Before I knew it," said Maggie, "the guest list was up to four hundred, the club had been reserved, and my mother had planned my spring vacation as a shopping tour of every bridal salon and china department in the area."

"It wasn't really her parents' fault," said Tom. "We never discouraged them from doing all the work while we were back in school. I guess we took it for granted that everything would be to our liking."

Maggie's parents married during World War II and never had what they called a real wedding. They wanted a lavish, opulent event for their daughter. From the beginning, communications had broken down, and Maggie and Tom had played a passive role.

"Up until the time of our big fight, I honestly thought my daughter and Tom expected us to go all out for their wedding," Maggie's mother confessed. "Maybe I got carried away, but at that point there was no conflict with what I thought they wanted."

"I was edgy and irritable with Tom, and when I suggested we elope, he blew up," said Maggie. "He said I was copping out and acting childish, and since I was so upset, he insisted that we fly home together and talk things over with my parents."

The communication gap narrowed considerably as Maggie and Tom clarified their ideas and wishes and stood firm on some details while acquiescing on others. The key to the eventual success of the wedding was their sensitivity to each other's feelings and those of their parents, as well as their ability to compromise on unimportant details.

Some marriage counselors believe that if a wedding is not planned by the couple themselves, they're apt to take the vows less seriously. So even if you agree to a family production, you should have a sense of control. And sometimes that means taking the reins away from your mother.

Let's be honest. Of course you love your mother, and you're grateful for all she's provided. But it's been a rocky road, too, starting with the first time you declared your independence. Mother and daughter relationships are enormously complicated and fraught with emotion, and your wedding could provoke some unpredictable behavior.

In her book, *My Mother, Myself,* Nancy Friday explains how her marriage made her feel particularly close to her mother, as if a new kind of bond had been established. "As I planned the details of the menu, the flowers, the ceremony, and the parties surrounding those days, I think I had her [mother's] pleasure in mind as much as Bill's and my own. It was our wedding . . . but for the first time in my life when a judgment of taste had to be made, I did it her way. The night before the wedding, I asked Bill to move out, not just to another room, but to a different hotel. While my mother was speeding forward to meet her adventurous daughter, I was retreating back to her."

As the wedding date approaches, brides often find themselves being drawn to their mothers. Some daughters want to be nurtured more, others want approval for their life decision. Still others are subconsciously telling their mothers, "See, I'm really like you after all." This common experience can erase a mother's fears. She can now worry less about her daughter's future, and she assumes the new role of confidante now that the war of independence is over. But is it?

As one bride recalled, "The night we were engaged, Mom brought me a present, a tradition that started with my older sisters. It was a treasured family heirloom, and we both felt so close and loving that we cried as if to wash away all the bad things about our relationship. It was only when I said, 'I'd like to wear flowers in my hair instead of a veil,' that the problems began. Once again we were locking horns in a battle of wills."

There is no doubt that problems in the parent-child relationship pop up again when wedding plans are announced. For mothers and fathers, a daughter's or a son's wedding is a highly charged moment, often tinged by the themes of abandonment and loss. But if you've always been independent from your parents, it's unlikely that you'll turn into a puppet now. And parents need to realize that the more you make your own decisions, the more credit they get for having provided you with the strength to deal with the milestones of your life. Psychologists Mildred Newman and Bernard Berkowitz, authors of *How to Be Your Own Best Friend,* think that the main job of a parent is to help a child separate and live his or her own life. "If parents can't let a child go because they're unprepared for the experience, they're in trouble. If they've done their job well, the wedding will represent *their* success as well as the child's."

I suppose this sounds as if parents are the bad guys whose sole function is to undermine their daughter's wedding, let alone her happiness. Indeed, some brides with particular parental problems might have a very different approach. Her parents may not be hosting the ceremony and reception; may not be giving the bride away; may not be footing the bill; may not be in control of the guest list; may not even be invited!

Still, the bride who wants her wedding to include her parents has to be aware of their doubts, their depressions, and their dreams. It is just possible that your wedding will be a poignant reminder that they're getting older. They may perceive it as your final step in leaving home and thus feel useless and unwanted. Like other rituals, weddings can be a symbol of the life cycle moving on, the creation of a new generation. (Do they really want to think of themselves as potential grandparents?) Anything that juxtaposes one's own position in life with someone else's can be threatening, so even if your parents are totally graceful throughout this period, don't believe for a minute that their feelings aren't percolating with apprehension and tension.

In a last-ditch effort to keep control, for example, they may become too involved with your life and your wedding plans. Or they may have an instinct to abdicate all responsibility without seeking that heavenly middle ground of cooperation and compromise. This all-or-nothing approach is difficult to reconcile. In order to find the middle ground, the parent must see the child as an adult, and the child must understand the parent as a person. If you both think of this marriage as an opportunity to develop a new long-term relationship together, you may be joyfully surprised by the results.

Some parents have particularly odd reactions. There's the mother who finally loses the ten extra pounds, gets a new hairdo and a fabulous dress, and tries to upstage her daughter by looking as youthful and sensational as possible. She's hoping that the strangers who pass through the receiving line will say, "You look like sisters," but what she's thinking is, I'm not a mother anymore—I'm no longer needed.

If you're an only child or the last one to leave the nest, your parents might be afraid to face each other and their marriage, especially if "the children" have provided the reason for the marriage to continue. A number of brides confided that their parents' marriages ended not long after their own began.

As you plan this joyful rite of passage with your parents, don't let anyone hide feelings behind the busywork of finding a caterer or hiring a band. Understand that there will be problems, not the least of which can be caused by the shrinking power of the dollar.

Here's the bottom line: if you pay for your wedding, you get to make the decisions. If parents pay, they have the say. But, since no one wants to come to that kind of stark formulation, if you're footing the bill, and you know that, ultimately, you can call the tune, you'll probably back away from it. You don't want to punish your parents by shutting them out with your financial power, nor do your parents want to whip you into place with their purse strings. Either way, there will be compromises, but if you're accepting financial help, you should do so on the condition that you'd like final approval of the plans.

There are lots of ways to make it work. Let's say the one thing you care most about for your wedding is the dress you'll wear. Your mother has always thought of you in hand-clipped Alencon lace with pearls and a train that doesn't stop. If you like the idea, terrific. Accept the thousand-dollar dress gracefully, and wear it like a queen. But if you've always imagined yourself in a simple chiffon dress and a big picture hat, save your money and buy it yourself.

You and your fiancé should decide what's most important about your wedding before you tell your parents you're getting married. The ceremony itself should be your own expression of commitment in accordance with religious and civil law. And if you have a passion about that three-piece combo instead of the band that played at your parents' twenty-fifth anniversary, pay for it yourself. Some people think that even if you and your fiancé can't pay for the entire wedding, you should make some financial contribution for the occasion. "I spent a few hundred of my own dollars filling the reception hall with candles," one bride explained. "Mother thought the idea was frivolous and, no doubt, was worried about the added expense. But the room was beautiful, and I was really proud that I did it myself."

The old joke about the father secretly wishing that his daughter will elope is not that funny. Hosting an elegant party for any occasion can be a major financial burden, yet a lot of parents are afraid to deny their children a big wedding with all the trimmings. Some parents think their daughters have high expectations. And some parents, feeling pressure from peers or professional associates, will go into debt to host a lavish wedding they clearly can't afford. Obviously this is a big mistake, especially at a time when the economy is uncertain and interest rates are soaring.

Your job, and your fiancé's, is to discuss openly the resources your families can provide for this wedding and to plan accordingly.

Once you know what to expect from your family, you have to set your plans in motion. Since you probably work, manage an apartment, and have a social life, it won't be easy to handle the details of your wedding without help. The idea is to delegate as much responsibility as possible to people you trust, especially your maid or matron of honor, and, of course, your mother.

It isn't easy to ask friends or relatives to give up precious leisure time to help you with your wedding, and you must give them room to decline gracefully. Let's say you've decided to have your reception at the nicest restaurant you can find. You can think of three places that might accommodate the seventy-five guests you plan to invite, but you need someone to phone the owners, find out if the room is available, inquire about menus, prices, decorations, seating space, and sit-down or buffet dinners.

If you think a friend would be interested in the project, ask her if she has the time or if she knows of someone who might. If she says yes, you'll be free to shop around for a church or chapel while she handles the reception. If she says no, reassure her that it's not a big problem, and invite her to call you with any ideas she may have for the wedding.

One of the classic dilemmas is concentrating exclusively on the small details while the big decisions are left hanging. One bride admitted, "I wanted my wedding to be original and different, and I wound up spending hours deciding on the containers for the table arrangements. I got so bogged down I forgot to order the cake!"

Another woman remembered the shock of recognition when the

romantic adventure of getting married became a crash course in business management: "There were hundreds of practical business decisions to make, and I wound up creating a staff of people to help with each project. I think planning a wedding could qualify you to be the president of General Motors."

Some men have the following attitude: "It's really the bride's day. The groom wears black and fades into the woodwork. The bride wears something that draws all eyes." Or: "Some of us just resent planning a wedding for a whole year; you could resolve the energy crisis in less time than that." Or: "The most offensive thing about weddings is that they're not for the bride and groom, but for the parents' friends. You walk into the reception to the strains of 'Stardust,' and you search around desperately for a familiar face."

Maybe it's true that your future husband only has eyes for you and isn't terribly concerned or interested in the production of a wedding. But many people think that the premarriage period could reveal the relationship. If the groom abdicates responsibility for the wedding, he might be apathetic throughout the marriage. Who's active, who's passive, who will get her or his way—all these precedents might be set during this period of planning.

One way of involving your man is this: make a list of all the chores that need to be done and let him decide which he wants to do and when. Just be sure that you agree on deadlines. If he has a gourmet palate, he may want to plan the menu. If he likes music and photography, he'll want to be in charge. And once all the chores are divided, assume that he's responsible, and avoid the danger of nagging him every other day.

If he still has no interest, try to find out why he's resisting the idea of planning this party. As one groom explained, "Janet wanted a storybook wedding. I thought I didn't care, so I adopted a neutral position. I'd do nothing to kill the ideas she had, but I wasn't about to participate, either. I allowed myself to be carried along in her tide, but I didn't help her. We had fights and arguments to the point where we almost called it off. In the five years we were together, it was the most traumatic time."

Janet recalled feeling stranded, betrayed, and angry. "I was livid with Mark. Trying to get him to give me a guest list was like getting Russia to vote for civil rights." But one of her mistakes was not really asking Mark what he thought about her ideas. She made the decisions and expected him to carry them out. The result was that Mark felt alienated and decided to drop out.

"I don't believe any man who claims he doesn't care what happens at his own wedding," says Eric Margenau. "That kind of statement is a defense against his feelings. He might be avoiding conflict and trying not to make waves."

Consider this irony: the couple believes in marriage as an equal partnership, yet she plans all the details of the reception. They go to the trouble of creating a nonsexist ceremony, editing the vows to eliminate obedience, subservience, and any other medieval notion of marriage, but at the reception, he feels and acts like one of the guests, just going through the motions.

Mildred Newman and Bernard Berkowitz agree: "A contemporary man probably wants to participate in the wedding. It should be a sharing experience as much as the marriage." If either you or your man are leaving the decisions of your wedding up to someone else, you may be robbing yourselves of a chance to cooperate on something that might give you an indication of how your marriage will work in the long run. Maybe he'll never honestly care about a wedding and reception as much as he'll care about the first house you own, but his ideas and instincts shouldn't be ignored. Just don't expect him to share your illusions along with the work.

Liberated mamas aren't buying too many dolls for their daughters nowadays, but you probably owned one called Barbie or some equivalent clone. After Barbie came Ken, and both had wardrobes that guided your imagination out of the closet and into the realm of active fantasy. Barbie and Ken went to school together, shopped together at the supermarket, swam at the beach, and ultimately, got married. Like all good mythical Disneyesque fairies, she had a special white dress. He had a funny suit and a tall hat. They were always most beautiful and perfect in their marriage costumes, and you devised a whole scenario to fit the occasion. It was the beginning of your dream wedding.

One reader wrote the following to *Modern Bride* magazine: "Help! I found the perfect dress in your magazine, but none of the stores in my area has it." Tucked inside the envelope was a dog-eared page from the magazine dating back to 1974, when the prospective bride was 15 years old.

In *The Eternal Bliss Machine,* Marcia Seligson writes, "It's the old

Cinderella mythology. While little boys are dreaming heroic dreams of conquering worlds, little girls are yearning for transformation—becoming beautiful, becoming a woman, becoming a mommy. As marriage is the single event which will presumably guarantee that metamorphosis, it is, naturally, the day for which her entire life has been in preparation."

The primitive idea that a woman's real life begins on her wedding day helped propagate these fantasies by making the wedding a victorious symbol in a woman's life. In the not so distant past, old maids and spinsters were as much a threat to a woman's well-being as another world war. No wonder that a father was apt to spend more money for his daughter's wedding than for her education. And even though contemporary attitudes about marriage and the family have changed in favor of the independent woman, there can be a "once upon a time" spillover that causes a bride to make the idea of the wedding more important than the reality of the marriage.

Some women subconsciously believe that a wedding is so magical it will "cure" an ailing relationship. One classic notion: "He won't drink as much after we're married." The result: she spends the next ten years trying to rehabilitate her alcoholic husband. Like having a baby in order to save a marriage that should have ended years ago, it just doesn't work. Said one bride, "I thought for sure that being married would make Jack realize that I was truly loyal and devoted to him. I thought the jealous rages would stop as soon as the magic wand beknighted us into matrimony. They didn't stop. They changed from fits of verbal abuse into physical assaults. For him, the marriage was a license to beat me up."

More typically, a bride will be swept away by the idea of being a star for the first time in her life. Although some women are terrified of the spectacle and suffer all the classic symptoms of stage fright, others get caught up in the fantasy of being queen for a day. For this kind of bride, the postwedding crash can be devastating. If you really believe that this is the best day of your entire life, of course you are going to feel lousy when it's over.

To compensate for this depression, women sometimes throw themselves into the next life stage in a frantic effort to maintain some semblance of the prewedding excitement. They may furiously decorate their new home, have a baby right away, or simply get into a social whirl of dinner parties and nights on the town that will keep the adrenaline flowing.

Psychologists agree that one is apt to feel empty at the completion of any milestone in life. In this sense, a wedding is an ending as well as a beginning, and it can provoke despair when you feel that you're settling into a humdrum phase of life. To overcome it, you must recognize that there are exciting, challenging things to do in your life on an ongoing basis.

Having some romantic illusions about your wedding is both natural and desirable. Avoiding them totally can be as harmful as embracing them completely. There are women who are so afraid of their wedding fantasies that they bottle up their emotions, planning everything by the book regardless of individual tastes or wishes. For these brides, the dream wedding is so threatening that they will suppress their joy for fear of becoming overwhelmed by it. Said one woman, a successful publicist in the film industry, "With typical confidence and efficiency, I planned our wedding as if it were an important film premiere party. I read every etiquette book, contacted the caterers and the musicians to research who was best for the job, sent out the invitations, etc. About three weeks before the wedding, I realized that I wasn't doing this to impress the studio head at Twentieth Century. This was for me, and I finally allowed myself to revel in total happiness."

You probably think there's something terribly unfair about all of this. When half your friends are getting divorced, you've just made the courageous decision to marry. You've lived together long enough to adjust to each other's eccentricities (and what a job that was), and you've decided to bite the bullet and plan a future that will be bound by the commitment of marriage. How ironic that a wedding doesn't automatically pull together all the forces of peace and harmony, love and goodwill that should accompany such a momentous occasion.

Yet it can do all of that. Marriage is, after all, a ritual of affirmation. It inspires optimism, appeals to our sense of order and tradition, and is one of the life passages that can be celebrated rather than mourned.

The bride who suffers undue stress and disappointment is usually only dimly aware of the emotions that swirl about a wedding. If you can anticipate emotional reactions, you will spare yourself and others a lot of tension. It's like going away to college for the first time. You're more frightened if you don't know what a dormitory looks like. For most of us, familiarity breeds contentment, allowing us to enjoy the more subtle pleasures and rewards.

Maybe the saddest part about getting married is this: so many wonderful moments are concentrated in such a short period of time that you wish you could space them out for the rest of your life. Such as, a year later, when you're in bed with the flu—wouldn't it be fabulous if those crazy friends, the ones who had everyone at the rehearsal dinner doubled over in laughter with their testimonial version of "When I'm Sixty-Four," gathered round your sickbed for just one more chorus. And the time your brother, a cynic whose bah-humbug approach to weddings always made you furious, swallowed his pride and his tears and told you how absolutely happy he was for you both. And when your mother revealed that she had just finished making the most extraordinary wedding-ring quilt you'd ever seen and she hoped it would fit in with the decorating scheme.

Getting married *is* a time to rejoice, a time to embrace the people you love most. And don't be embarrassed if for the first time in years you start to feel a tiny bit sentimental about the whole thing.

2 · Getting Organized

Whether you've given yourselves a month or a year to plan a wedding that's simple or grand, a system of organization is necessary. The purpose is to make order out of chaos and to provide yourself with an instant reference to what needs to be done, when it should be ready, how much it costs, etc.

The first thing you need is a notebook. I like the idea of a well-bound ruled book that can be carried in a purse or briefcase, but if you have a passion for index cards or love the look of a loose-leaf, use it instead. The notebook or folder should be divided into three parts: (1) people, places, and things; (2) guests and gifts; and (3) a planning calendar.

People, Places, and Things

In order to make the system work, you have to learn how to budget your time as well as your money. To begin with, call the merchants (caterers, florists, etc.) who have been recommended by friends or whose advertisements appealed to you. Find out as much as you can about prices and services, and let them know that you are shopping around. If they think you are a smart consumer, they won't be tempted to charge higher rates or send you their junior apprentice. In some cases, the person you meet with at first won't be the one who'll actually perform the service. Make sure that you speak directly with the photographer or flower designer you will be working with to let them know your preferences.

Once you've narrowed down each field to two or three possibilities, call back to set up appointments. Ask in advance how long a conference might take, and schedule as many meetings as you can for other services in the same location. Get companies to send you brochures or any printed material available. If you're making a deposit against the total cost of the service, be sure to pay by check made out to the name of the firm or individual—never to cash. And get a receipt.

In every case, if you're buying goods or services, you should follow standard guidelines that will protect you against price gouging, unreliability, misrepresentation, and misunderstandings. Aside from shopping around to compare prices, you should confirm your arrangements in writing and read all contracts carefully. Keep copies of letters, contracts, brochures, and other service information in a separate file or envelope. Let your notebook be your personal wedding planner. The following illustrations show you one way to organize a formal wedding. If your own wedding plans are simpler, delete or change the information accordingly. In addition to the charts on the following pages, you may want to set up separate ones for beauty and health, legal and financial, or anything else that will help you with the details of your particular wedding. If you will be changing your name, you'll need to order new checks and deposit forms. If you're starting off in a new house or apartment, magazine subscriptions, utility bills, store charges, and other monthly mail should be forwarded to your new address.

Printed Materials

From the wedding invitations themselves to the stationery you'll use to write your thank-you notes, you'll want to shop carefully and wisely. You may decide, for example, to have a prestigious stationer engrave your invitations and announcements, but you might not be willing to pay their prices for notepaper and informals. You can buy personal stationery "by the pound" in a variety of colors and have your name and address printed rather than engraved.

When you order your invitations, many stationers will try to sell you printed matchbooks, swizzle sticks, place cards, and even coat-check tags. Understand that these unnecessary personalized items are not so much a tradition as they are an incremental sale.

Keep in mind that the post office has strict size requirements for letters. If the envelopes are too small, the post office computers and sorting machines won't be able to process them. If they're oversized,

Printed Material

CATEGORY	SERVICE COMPANY	REPRESENTATIVE	ADDRESS PHONE	ESTIMATED COST	ACTUAL COST	CONFIRMING LETTER	ORDERED/DUE	NOTES
Invitations (rec. cards) (pew cards) (reply cards)	Tiffany	John Smith	57th/5th 755-8000	$250	$265	yes 1/3	12/5 2/5	110 order
Announcements	"	"	"	$200	$216	"	" "	"
At-home cards								
Personal stationery letter paper informals memo pads pocket pads	The Paper-works	Mary Coe	555-3724 125 Houston	$100		yes, receipt	1/27 2/27	
Xeroxed maps	The Copy Cat	Harry	86 N. Franklin	$5.25				Harry says instant . . . give him a day
Change-of-address cards	post office		33rd/8th	—	—	—	—	
Extras matches place cards cake boxes	—	—	—	—	—	—	—	
Stamps	post office			$36.00	$36.00			get pretty ones
Calligraphy	—	—	—	—	—	—	—	

you'll have to pay additional postage. Even if your supplier doesn't know the requirements, you should. No envelope should be smaller than 3½ inches high and 5 inches long. This rule affects the size of some informal notepaper. Check with the post office before mailing invitations or announcements.

If Xeroxed maps are to be included, enter the cost of preparing them in your notebook.

The Ceremony

One of the first things you'll need to decide is what kind of ceremony you want to have, and when and where. Try to avoid scheduling your wedding on a major holiday weekend such as Labor Day or Memorial Day. People plan family outings or combine that time with vacations, and they may resent going to a wedding on a weekend they've looked forward to for months.

When you meet with your clergyman or officiant, you'll want to know what choices you have for a traditional or nontraditional service, whether you can write your own vows, etc. Don't be shy about expressing your preferences. If you've always wanted your sister to sing a hymn in her operatic voice, see if it's okay. Most officiants will do what they can to tailor the service to your tastes.

Look around the church, chapel, or chambers and determine how the space can be spruced up for the wedding. Would a potted palm brighten that drab corner? Perhaps colorful baskets of flowers could be placed at the altar. Find out what's allowed and what's not, and cross-index the information to the flowers and plants page of your notebook.

Now is also the time to inquire about ceremony fees and donations. Don't be embarrassed to ask your clergyman what the customary fees are for the church or synagogue, the organist, the sexton, and the ceremony itself. Find out, too, if there are any restrictions on the use of flashbulbs, tapes, cameras, rice, rose petals, candles, or anything else you may want to have at your wedding. If a rehearsal is required, write it in your notebook.

Wedding Clothes

Since most traditionally styled wedding dresses are special ordered, you ought to choose your dress twelve to sixteen weeks before the wedding so that there will be time for fittings and alterations.

Ceremony

DATE____ PLACE ____ TIME ____ ADDRESS ________

CATEGORY	SERVICE COMPANY	REPRESENTATIVE	ADDRESS PHONE	ESTIMATED COST	ACTUAL COST	CONFIRMING LETTER	ORDERED/DUE	NOTES
Church	St. Mary's	Mrs. Smith	Main St. 432-6756	$200		yes 9/12		
Clergyperson or officiant	Father John		"	$100				discuss ceremony changes
Sexton		"		$ 25				
Organist				$ 50				
Soloist				—	—			
Attendants:								Mary and Joan said yes; Ann might be in Europe
bridesmaid								
bridesmaid								
maid of honor								
Jeweler	Rose's Gold	Mr. Simpson	110 Elm 468-7452	$400		yes	9/13-10/4	Inc. engraving on Tom's ring
Rehearsal								Fri/Dec. 4
Extras								
rice				$ 3.				
pew ribbons				—	—			
candles				$10.				
aisle carpet				—	—			
Decorations								See Plants & Flowers

Wedding Clothes

CATEGORY	SERVICE COMPANY	REPRESEN-TATIVE	ADDRESS PHONE	ESTIMATED COST	ACTUAL COST	CONFIRMING LETTER	ORDERED/DUE	NOTES
My dress	Bee's Bridal	Susan Wolf	Paramus Mall 476-4724	$550		yes 1/30	1/30 4/30	$100 dep. Fitting: 3/15
Headpiece	"	"	"	$100				Deposit: $25
Maid of honor Bridesmaids	"	"	"	$100 each		"	1/30 4/15	get sizes before 2/10
John's suit ushers, dads	Martin's Formalwear	Max Loos	York St. 555-2089	$50 each		yes 3/15	3/15 5/5	check accessories
Mom								wants to wear a tea-length print
Clothes for Honeymoon trip								don't forget to buy a new swimsuit

Permanent Records

CATEGORY	SERVICE COMPANY	REPRESENTATIVE	ADDRESS PHONE	ESTIMATED COST	ACTUAL COST	CONFIRMING LETTER	ORDERED/DUE	NOTES
Photographer	Say Cheese	John Smith	555-3876 Rte. 22	$350		yes, 5/8 contract rec. 5/22		20 pix (8 x 10) in leather album. 20 4 x 5 prints in guest book. Each additional print, $10
Tape recordings	Uncle John	—	555-9476	—	—	—		
Video tape	TV Time	Mary Brown	Rte. 22 555-6735	$750				can be edited later for $200. dep. req. Don't think I'll do it
Films	Bobby							says he wants to use new Super-8
Polaroid	Sally		555-9736					wants to make us an instant album—her wedding gift

Bridesmaid dresses, though simpler in detail and styling, are also made to order, and if your attendants cannot make personal appearances at the bridal salon, you must provide their sizes and full measurements. (See the size chart, page 115.)

If you wear a size 8 or 10, you might be able to buy a sample dress from your bridal shop, and if you do, the dress may need cleaning or repairing. Some salons "stock" dresses in different sizes and have expert seamstresses on the premises to make alterations and create a perfect fit, but don't count on it. It's not a common practice.

If your fiancé and his attendants are going to rent formal suits for the occasion, they should make arrangements at least one month in advance of the wedding.

Use your notebook to record names, dates, and costs. Jot down any thoughts you have on style, color, or accessories.

Permanent Records

From standard print photographs to microcassette tape recordings, new technological advances in pictures and sound make it easier than ever to record your wedding. If you decide to supplement your photographs with a tape or film, find out what's involved. Will your reception turn into a stage set for equipment, wires, and cameramen, or will a simple battery-operated porta-pack be all that's necessary? From the kind of lighting that's required to how long the tape or film will run, you should pin down all the details before you make a big investment.

It's possible that one multimedia enterprise will supply all the recording services you want, but chances are you'll have to meet with specialists in each area. Start with telephone inquiries about costs, services, and availability. Then set up appointments to review their work before you close the deal.

Flowers and Plants

A florist alone might not be able to meet all your wedding needs, especially if you want to rent some potted palms or buy pots of flowers. Sure, they'll get you anything you want, but they'll probably get it from the local nursery and have to charge you more than if you went to the nursery yourself.

If you don't know the difference between an anemone and a carnation, do some preliminary research by contacting your local botanical

Flowers and Plants

CATEGORY	SERVICE COMPANY	REPRESEN-TATIVE	ADDRESS PHONE	ESTIMATED COST	ACTUAL COST	CONFIRMING LETTER	ORDERED/DUE	NOTES
Bouquets	Daisy May	May Marlow	195 First St. 563-4725	$100		yes, 5/8	5/8 6/22	call re streamer
Corsages	"	"	"	50		"	"	
Boutonnieres	"	"	"	15		"	"	
Pews	"	"	"	60		"	"	
Altar	"	"	"			"	"	real azalea plants
Trees	ABC Nursery	Bob White	Henry St. 673-6729	100	100	yes, 5/10	5/10 6/21	6 ficus trees for church hall del. & pickup inc.
Centerpieces	"	"	"	100	100	"	"	10 double begonia plants in clay pots
Dried flowers								
Silk flowers								

garden or garden club. They will have books and brochures, as well as flowers in bloom, and you can find out what will be in season during the month of your wedding.

When you meet with your florist or nursery salesperson, she or he will automatically assume that you want the standard nuptial arrangements. Bring photographs from magazines and books if you want to duplicate a bouquet or centerpiece.

Aside from flowers for the ceremony and reception, you may want flowers for your rehearsal dinner; you may consider sending your parents a silk or dried permanent flower arrangement as a thank-you; or your fiancé may want a single rose in a bud vase in your hotel room. Plan it all now, get the prices set, and then confirm everything when you're absolutely sure about the details.

The Reception

It is the little details that will make the difference for the reception. I recently went to a wedding celebration at a lovely restaurant. The tables were set beautifully, the music was terrific, and the food delicious. It seemed that nothing was overlooked, until I went to the ladies' room to freshen up. No one thought to put bars of real hand soap at the sink, and the towel dispenser could have been supplemented with individual paper tea towels or, better yet, linen guest towels. Let your notebook jog your memory on small things like this. Jot down your ideas whenever they come to you.

Remember that you, your immediate family, and your attendants might arrive late for the reception because photographs are being taken. Make a note to ask a friend to greet people, ask them to sign the guest book, and help them find their seats.

If you want to have a separate record of the songs the band will play, or the menu itself, use a page in your notebook to record the particulars.

Menu

Hors d'Oeuvres

pâté on sesame rounds
crab claws with anchovy dip
crudités with cheese dip
assorted canapés

Reception

CATEGORY	SERVICE COMPANY	REPRESEN-TATIVE	ADDRESS PHONE	ESTIMATED COST	ACTUAL COST	CONFIRMING LETTER	ORDERED/DUE	NOTES
Place	Country Club	Mr. Phelps	Grove St. 847-3769	$300		yes, 3/18		they provide linens, place settings, glasses
Food	Martha's Catering	Martha Jones	8th & Main 674-4797	$2,500		yes, 3/20		100 @ $25 per head. Inc. cold hors d'oeuvres and service
Bar	Country Club	Mr. Phelps	same	$500				open bar, 1 hr. champagne wine inc.
Cake	The Eclair	Ms. Adams	12th & Main 673-8764	$100		yes, 3/28		2-tiered chocolate
Music		Joan Woods	874-6749	$50		yes, 4/6		will play harp 1 hr.
	Woody Post Trio	Woody Post	785-4789	$300		yes, 4/6		3 hrs.
Extras candles				$25				Aunt Mary will set up
soaps towels coat check								Mr. Phelps will handle Inc. in cost

Buffet

chilled salmon in dill sauce
sliced roast beef au jus
marinated snow peas with sliced almonds
scalloped potatoes

Dessert

wedding cake
mixed fresh fruit
coffee

Transportation and Travel

This section in your notebook can include everything from how you get to the church and the reception to honeymoon travel arrangements. Whether you hire a limousine, a horse and carriage, or drive your own moped, you should make sure that everything will be ready to go on time. Don't forget that a special traffic officer might be needed for the church or reception area to direct traffic and parking. Or you might want to arrange for valet parking for guests.

Out-of-town guests usually pay for their own arrangements. Have your travel agent book local accommodations in their names, or make available a list of transportation options from their hometowns. Keep an updated record of this information.

Even though the groom traditionally makes the honeymoon arrangements, if you're planning your wedding and trip together, put all the particulars in the notebook.

Guests and Gifts

The second major section of your notebook should be a list of the guests and a record of the gifts they've sent. The guest list should show at a glance who's coming and who's not. The gift column describes the item and shows whether a thank-you note has been sent. I like the idea of a number code for gifts to avoid any errors. It works like this: buy a double set of stick-on numbers from your stationery store. Place a number on the opened gift, and place the corresponding number in

Transportation and Travel

CATEGORY	SERVICE COMPANY	REPRESEN-TATIVE	ADDRESS PHONE	ESTIMATED COST	ACTUAL COST	CONFIRMING LETTER	ORDERED/DUE	NOTES
Limousines	Ajax Car	Norma Hull	Madison St. 684-7836	2 @ $40 each		yes, 6/12	6/12 7/15	will arr. ½ hr. before ceremony
Cars (ours)								parked at club for getaway
Planes Trains Buses	Flash Travel Agency	Jackie Borden	784-7827 Jermain Ave.					is getting schedules from Boston to Pittsburgh
Honeymoon plane	"	"	"	$1,000				seats conf. rd. trip
Car rental	Avis	Wizard	894-8483	(check)				
Hotel	Flash Travel	JB				yes, 4/10		requested view of ocean
Valet parking	Country Club	Mr. Phelps		$25				

the notebook next to the name of the person who sent it. If you've received three Waterford decanters, you'll know that Uncle John sent the one with the cut crystal top.

Although it is not considered proper for guests to bring gifts to the reception, some always do, and you should designate a secure area for them. If that area is a coat-check room, the attendant will be responsible for the gifts. If your wedding is at home, ask a friend or relative to accept the gifts for you, and to put them in a safe place. Record these details.

GUESTS	PHONE	RSVP	GIFTS	NO.	THANK-YOUS
Mr. & Mrs. Eric Green 201 Bayville Dr. Albuquerque, New Mexico 87103	505-555-2134	yes	Waterford decanter	1	sent 3/15
Ms. Janet Lieberman 42 W. Highland Santa Fe, N.M. 87501	505-354-8649	yes	Martex sheets	2	sent 3/30
Mr. James Lardner 25 Madison St. Houston, Texas 77001	713-621-8585	no	table saw	3	

A Planning Calendar

The third section of your notebook should be a calendar, so that you can have a quick view of all your appointments, meetings, phone calls to make on certain days, checks that should be mailed at a particular time, etc. If you like the style of seeing an entire month at a glance, construct it that way. Otherwise, make it a weekly calendar.

On the following pages you will find a three-month timetable for planning the wedding.

Quick Reference List for Brides and Grooms

Three months (or more) before your wedding:

1. Decide what kind of wedding you want, and where and when you want to have it.

2. Contact your officiant to see if he or she is available; set the date.

3. Determine your budget and guest list.

4. Reserve your reception area and caterer. If it's going to be at home, arrange for cleaning and repairs. If it's in a garden, rent the tents and tables, hire a gardener now to trim hedges one week before the wedding.

5. Investigate and decide on florists and nurseries, photographers and video services, musicians or tape systems.

6. Select your attendants, and ask them if they're available.

7. Order your invitations and announcements.

8. Make an appointment with a bridal salon to order your wedding dress, accessories, and bridesmaid outfits. Or start looking at ready-to-wear selections.

9. If you're registering for gifts, select your patterns and fill in your preferences.

10. Make transportation arrangements.

11. If the wedding is planned in a resort community during high season, book accommodations now.

Two months ahead:

1. Go over all the details for the reception, including the following: (a) physical layout, (b) menus, (c) seating arrangements, (d) parking, (e) bar, and (f) wedding cake.

2. If possible, arrange for bridesmaids to have fittings on their dresses.

3. Select and order the menswear.

4. Check on your dress alterations.

5. Start addressing invitations.

6. Purchase or order gifts for your attendants.

7. Set up hair and makeup appointments for day of your wedding; make appointments for facials, saunas, or massages for the week before.

8. Make any medical or dental appointments.

One month to go:

1. Mail invitations.

2. Send out wedding announcement to newspapers.
3. Buy any new clothes you'll need for the honeymoon.
4. Get blood tests and license.
5. Have final consultations with service people.
7. Take your mother out to lunch, just the two of you.
8. Plan the rehearsal dinner.
9. Have announcements ready to mail.
10. Make sure rings are ready and engraved, if desired.
11. If you're assuming your husband's name, change your driver's license, charge accounts, insurance policies, etc.
12. If you're moving, notify the post office and send in change-of-address forms to magazines, etc.
13. If your husband will be your beneficiary (and vice versa), make sure all insurance policies say so.

3·
The Budget

Who Pays?

The old rules say that the bride and her family pay for almost all major wedding costs, an idea that followed logically from a social system that encouraged men to support and be responsible for women. In paying for the wedding, the father of the bride was offering a kind of dowry to the man who would be assuming the financial burden of his daughter. A wedding meant gifts for the couple—usually household items—which gave the new husband a financial head start in furnishing a home. In *The Money Motive,* author Thomas Wiseman explains that "the bride-price and the dowry have been features of the marriage rites among Semites, Babylonians, Chinese, Japanese, Africans, Polynesians, Eskimos, aborigine Australians. These customary payments have their modern equivalent in the form of wedding presents, or wedding payments."

The notion that the bride was property and could be bought for the right price fell out of favor along with arranged marriages. Yet, until quite recently, the bride's parents paid for the wedding and "gave" the woman over to the new man. It seemed fair enough. The groom's parents had presumably already spent a great deal of money educating and preparing their son to become a breadwinner. In return for being cared for by her new husband, the bride would run the household and raise the children.

For some modern couples, the traditional system is still preferred. But for those who subscribe to a new ideal of social and economic equality, "who pays for what" at the wedding will no longer penalize the bride's father, who had also educated her and prepared her to become a breadwinner. That's why a lot of wedding expenses are now being shared by both families, or by the couple themselves.

Still, with unequal incomes, complicated divorces, and geographic separations among family members, it is not always practical to use one set standard for paying the bills. If only a dozen people from his family can make it from Montana to Miami for your big day, it's silly to expect them to pay half the costs of your large, lavish wedding. And if one family has megabucks and the other is waging a losing war against inflation, they can't be expected to share costs unless the wedding is on the modest side.

Some families don't want to split the bill and thereby relinquish control over the wedding plans or face the kind of bickering that can make everyone crazy. As one bride said, "The tension kept building between my mother and his. It was after the fight over whether to serve mock turtle soup or jellied madrilene that I stepped in. My in-laws would pay for the liquor and band; we would pay for the food and hotel."

There are fathers who feel insulted or hurt if their daughters do not accept the wedding as a gift and an act of love. The flip side of that is the parent who offers the cost of the wedding in any form the couple wishes to use it—buying a car, taking a fabulous trip, or buying furniture, to name a few. But no matter how you choose to pay for it all, you should be aware of the traditional breakdown of expenses. At *Modern Bride* magazine, we suggest this list of who pays for what.

The bride pays for:

1. The groom's wedding ring (if he wears one)
2. A wedding gift for the groom (optional)
3. Presents for the attendants (some couples pay for the dresses and tuxedo rentals in lieu of gifts)
4. Housing for out-of-town attendants
5. Her medical examination
6. Hair stylist, makeup artist (optional)

The groom pays for:

1. The marriage license
2. His medical examination
3. Wedding (engagement) rings
4. A gift for the bride (optional)

5. The bride's bouquet (bride's family may want to pay for this)
6. Boutonnieres for male attendants
7. Flowers for the mothers
8. Gloves, ascots, or ties for his attendants
9. Gifts for ushers and best man (again, their outfits may replace the gift)
10. Housing for out-of-town attendants
11. Bachelor dinner (optional)
12. Fee for the clergyman
13. The honeymoon (can be shared by couple)

The bride's family pays for:

1. The bride's wedding clothes and trousseau
2. Invitations and announcements
3. Engagement and wedding photographs
4. Rental for church, if any
5. Fees for the organist, soloist, or sexton
6. Aisle carpet and canopy
7. Flowers for church
8. Bridesmaids' bouquets
9. Transportation for bridal party from house to church to reception
10. Bridesmaids' luncheon (optional)
11. Entire cost of reception

The groom's family pays for:

1. Clothes for wedding
2. Any traveling expenses and hotel bills for themselves
3. Wedding gift for couple
4. Rehearsal dinner (sometimes paid for by the bride's family, or shared)

The attendants pay for:

1. Clothes for the wedding (unless couple chooses to pay)
2. Traveling expenses
3. Wedding gift for the couple

The guests pay for:

1. Traveling expenses, including hotel accommodations
2. Wedding gift

Alternatives

1. You and he pay for it all.
2. His family pays directly for the liquor and/or music.
3. You let your generous friends host the reception, and you pay the ceremony fees, etc. (In this case, do not insist that the food be prepared by the chef at the Four Seasons. And offer to pick up the cost of the champagne or the flowers. There's nothing worse than sending your hosts flowers the day after the wedding.)

How to Work Out a Budget

If you've always figured on getting to the church on time in an antique Rolls-Royce, budget your transportation costs higher than average, and cut back, if necessary, on the price of your invitations or flowers. Budgets are always determined by estimating necessary and optional expenditures. Wedding food, clothing, and shelter costs have to be set before you know how much is left for music, photographs, flowers, and the like.

Use the charts in your notebook as a guide to all budget expenses. Get tentative prices over the phone, in person, or from people who have bought the same services or goods; and make sure you record the information in the estimated cost columns. Underline or circle in red any items that can be changed in favor of a lower bottom line. For example, if the engraver has quoted two dollars per invitation, you might want to have them printed instead. Or the big black limousine might be eliminated by having your brother drive the family car. The following illustration can serve as a guide. A wedding for one hundred guests that costs $5,000 could be budgeted this way.

Invitations and announcements	$200
Photographs	300
Rehearsal dinner	250
Wedding dress and veil	500
Flowers	400
Transportation	100
Church fees	150
Reception	
food, beverage, service,	2,500
music	600
Total est. costs	$5,000

It's common for the reception to use up at least half the budget. But your own priorities might slice the pie differently. Want to spend $1,000 on your wedding dress?

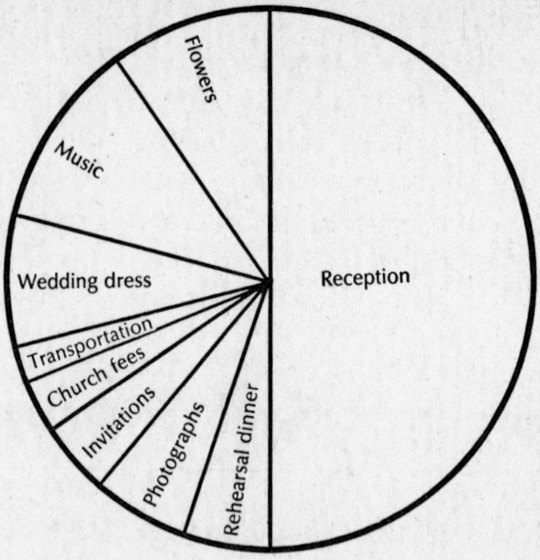

Bargains and Bargaining

Weddings are big business. They represent over twelve billion dollars in gross retail expenditures each year. There's not a florist or caterer or photographer around whose profits aren't enriched by other people's marriage vows. So you have some clout as a priority customer. The problem is, you're a novice in the field, or at best a one-time "repeat" customer. It is assumed, therefore, that you won't know how many white roses should be placed among the baby's breath in your fifty-dollar bouquet. And the engraver will try to sell you cake boxes, cocktail napkins, matches, coat-check tags, even pens and pencils with *Danny and Susie* stamped in gold. But even if he offers you 10 percent off for all the unnecessary paper, it's still no bargain.

If you want all these service people to respect your judgment, you'll have to impress them with your knowledge of their specialties. Then and only then will you understand why rubrum lilies cost more than carnations, or why engravers' fees are higher than printers' charges. When you buy a wedding dress, do you know the difference between silk organza, polyester organza, and Dacron sheer? And aside from the top-of-the-line silk tulle, could you recognize the various grades of nylon and polyester veiling that are available?

Wedding merchants don't expect you to be a smart shopper. They expect you to be romantic rather than wise, grateful rather than demanding. Your job, of course, is to get the best for the least, and sometimes that means striking a hard bargain.

Americans don't know the art of bargaining and often assume that all prices are fixed. But prices are based on markups which range from 50 to 150 percent of the wholesale cost, not including labor. Indeed, many merchants won't consider bargaining—especially department stores, chain stores, and prestigious specialty shops—but when you're ordering anything in volume, it is common to get a percentage discount. For example, some hotels or motels offer group rates for blocks of rooms if reservations are made well in advance. If you have to reserve a dozen or more rooms at the inn, don't ask what the rate will be. Ask if they offer a discounted rate for that many rooms. Always start negotiations in the hypothetical; i.e., "If I were to book 15 rooms at your hotel, would you offer a group-rate discount?" Depending on policy, they will say yes or no, and you can go on from there. If you don't ask, you might miss out on the 10 percent off for the rooms for your bridesmaids and ushers.

Make an anonymous phone call to the florist, and find out the cost of one centerpiece consisting of a dozen mixed bulb flowers (four irises, four freesias, four tulips, and a filler of candytuft or lemon leaves). Once you know the price of one arrangement, ask him what the cost for 20 would be, based on a volume order. If he says there is no discount, find another florist. Some florists will encourage you to share altar arrangements with another bride who is being married at the same church on the same day. If your florist doesn't know about any other weddings, ask your clergyman.

It is hard to negotiate discounts in some clubs and hotels where union rules and state liquor licenses limit the options of bringing in nonunion bands, your own supply of champagne, etc. But if your caterer offers to purchase all the liquor, he might be getting a markup for a service you could perform yourself.

Consumer Savvy

Whether you bargain for discounts or not, you should shop around for the best prices in town. Check with the Better Business Bureau if you want to know whether any complaints have been registered against a particular company from other brides or from professional people who have used caterers and florists for weddings or business entertainment. Insist on seeing, tasting, or listening to every possible detail. If the caterer recommends Pouilly-Fuissé for the fish course at ten dollars per bottle, be sure (a) that you like it, and (b) that you don't prefer a simple five-dollar Muscadet.

If you're booking rooms at a hotel, check each room individually to make sure that there is not too much street noise, an unsightly view, or limited space.

It pays to get it all in writing. If you're hiring Hot Lips Lanagan and his four-piece band, be sure that your contract specifies that Hot Lips himself shows up. Pin down the length of their breaks, whether they'll play during dinner, and the overtime charges, should they be necessary. Catering contracts should spell out the menu, the number of waiters, waitresses, bartenders, et al. Don't ever pay a bill that is not itemized; for example, "Reception—$1,000." Photography contracts should include the number of photographs to be selected from proofs, the delivery dates of proofs and finished prints, who owns the negatives, etc.

Never pay in full. Don't pay for any goods or services until they are delivered, although you can expect to pay a deposit to the caterer (or catering establishment), the florist, et al. If for any reason you have to cancel the contract, check your local government Consumer Protection office to see whether your state has consumer protection laws that allow you to get your money back, less a penalty for business lost or goods already paid for.

Use credit cards. If an establishment fails to deliver, American Express will battle it out for you. This applies especially to clothing stores, hotels, restaurants and clubs, and some florists. If deposits are required, always make out your check to the company or individual supplying the service, never to "cash."

4 · The Wedding

You can do it on skates in a roller disco, in a balloon floating over the countryside, or at a fabulous estate with a flock of pink flamingos around an Olympic-sized pool. You can have a "secret" marriage in such states as California, be part of a mass nuptial sponsored by the Playboy Club, or simply get into your car and elope. As long as you conform to state laws and can find a willing officiant, you can have any kind of wedding you want.

There are reports of everything—from a bridesmaid dress designed especially for a miniature poodle to ceremonies performed "on the road" and announced over the CB radio band. Some couples set the date in accordance with their most positive astrological periods or wait until their biorhythms say it's okay, but no matter how amusing, individual, or just plain silly a wedding can be, the seriousness of the moment shouldn't be overwhelmed by the staging.

Although most couples are returning to the idea of the traditional wedding, some like a more novel approach. As long as the ceremony is handled with taste and dignity, anything goes. Still, if the bride wears basic black or the best man's toast is a speech denouncing the use of nuclear energy, the wedding might be a failure. This is not the best time to satirize, politicize, or otherwise bore people with ideology.

I heard recently about what was called a "benefit" wedding. The couple were active members of a certain political organization, and the wedding guests were asked to make tax-free contributions to the cause in lieu of wedding gifts. One guest, who was outraged by the whole idea, said, "I'd have been insulted if they asked for a pledge to the heart association, let alone that group of political goofballs."

There's a fine line between doing it your way and showing total contempt for social standards and tradition. You might think it is fabulous to be married *au naturel* in a redwood tub, but your guests might be sorry they ever showed up. As you set out to plan the wedding that's right for you, let your social sensibility help you make the right decisions.

It makes sense to think of the wedding and reception as one idea. If you get married at a big cathedral with an elaborate dress and a dozen attendants and then wind up having a cocktail reception for 50 people, you haven't meshed the idea of your wedding. From free and easy to fabulous and formal, nuptial styles are no longer limited by rigorous social etiquette, but there are still some guidelines.

The Elopement

You know the idea. Just as the sun is beginning to set, you decide impulsively to drive off, and you arrive joyously at your destination at midnight. The white frame house is on a tree-lined street, and the picket fence almost hides the sign: Justice of the Peace. You ring the bell and the sleepy-eyed couple clad in nightshirts and stocking caps graciously welcome you to your home away from home. After they pronounce you husband and wife, you're offered a glass of sherry from the old dusty bottle, and with tears in their eyes the justice and his wife say their good-byes to the son and daughter they wished they'd had.

In reality, unless you're going to an all-night wedding chapel in Las Vegas, where instant marriages are big business, no self-respecting justice of the peace will be all that thrilled to be dragged out of bed in the middle of the night to perform a wedding service for a couple of strangers. Even an elopement needs planning, and in most states that includes having blood tests, obtaining a license, and calling the officiant in advance to make sure he or she is available.

Once all that is accomplished, you'll enjoy a simple civil ceremony, and you'll pay anywhere from fifteen to fifty dollars for the service. The officiant will provide witnesses who can sign the marriage certificate, or you can ask a couple of friends to join you instead. As always, it's a good idea to discuss the arrangements directly with the justice before going ahead.

How do you find a justice of the peace? If you have no firsthand recommendations from friends or family (or if you don't want to ask in order to keep the big secret), check the Yellow Pages. If you want to marry outside of your home state, the local telephone business office can provide you with access to out-of-state directories.

City Hall

In most states, City Hall ceremonies are performed on a first come, first served basis. Others will allow you to reserve time in advance. Usually, City Hall wedding chapels are closed, along with other municipal offices, on weekends and holidays. The City Hall wedding is probably the most pragmatic and the least romantic way to get married. In New York, the service is offered in English, Spanish, and French, and it takes about one minute; but you can no longer get the license and, in the same day, go across the hall to the chapel for the ceremony. Couples must wait twenty-four hours before tying the knot, and in order to get a license in the first place, you have to provide blood tests and physical examination records that are not less than 10 but not more than 30 days old.

Because the procedure is so simple and matter-of-fact, a lot of couples who want to skip the hoopla, as well as the cost of a larger wedding, prefer City Hall and its five-dollar fee to other choices. The bride can wear a special but simple street-length dress, and the groom a suit or sport jacket, with a boutonniere if he likes. Some chapels offer a separate photography service, but most allow couples to bring their own cameras. The "next in line" will usually agree to take a snapshot for you. One couple summed up the experience this way: "If you care about your wedding, don't go to City Hall. But if all you want is to be married, it's a good choice."

Wedding Chapels

These are packaged versions of the justice of the peace, found primarily in California and the Southwest. The buildings themselves are often embellished with cupids, wedding bells, or neon signs to identify their purpose. Ceremonies can cost as little as twenty-five dollars for the basic wedding ritual or as much as five thousand dollars for the works (which might include videotapes or photographs and a wedding dress). In some states you may truly have an "instant" marriage at one of these chapels without applying for a license or having blood tests or physical exams.

In California, Montana, and Texas, for example, the Confidential

Marriage Act simply requires that couples complete a certificate (cost—five dollars) and say an appropriate "I do." There is no public record of the marriage, and except for a request by the couple themselves, the certificate can only be seen by court order. Without a doubt, it's one of the easiest ways to wed, but proceed with caution. Blood tests and physical exams shouldn't be dismissed too easily, since they screen for rubella and venereal disease.

The Judge

If you know a judge, he or she might agree to marry you in chambers or at some other location. Couples who prefer a female officiant are apt to choose a judge, since qualified female clerics are harder to find. A judge is not duty bound to perform a wedding ceremony, and there is usually no fixed fee attached to the service. As such, an offer of fifty to seventy-five dollars is reasonable. Some judges will request that the fee be donated in their name to a local charity.

The Rectory Wedding

If you want a religious ceremony without walking down the aisle, you may be able to marry in the rectory of your church. If the clergyman is a friend of the family, he will probably not perform the service without permission from your parents. If you or your fiancé are respectable members of the congregation in your own right, there is usually no problem. Fees to the clergyman or the church for this simplified religious ritual range from twenty-five to fifty dollars.

Postscript to a Private Wedding

There's often some emotional fallout from a private wedding or elopement. Typically, families will feel rejected, and friends will feel slighted; hurt feelings might be expressed by direct confrontation or a simple cold shoulder. Yet, knowing all this, some couples can't imagine taking their wedding vows publicly. One bride put it this way: "I don't agree that it's antisocial to have a private wedding ceremony. Not all rites of passage are open to the public. When you deliver a baby, for instance, you don't invite a hundred people to witness the birth." And a recently married man, whose second wedding was a brief trip to City Hall, said, "At my age, I'm not doing anything momentous for anyone else. The wedding was for me and my wife. At this age, you understand what it is you owe others and what you owe yourself."

Still, an exclusive wedding ceremony doesn't preclude a more public celebration later. Most couples who opt for a private wedding either host their own postnuptial party or are honored by friends or families who cooperate on a reception. Sending out wedding announcements is a perfect way to formalize such an event.

The next step from total privacy usually involves not more than a dozen people. The ceremony can be performed by a civil officiant at his or her respective establishment or at a private home. A religious service in a rectory, a chapel, or at home might also be arranged. It's likely that you will want to celebrate with a larger group following the ceremony or at a later date, and wedding announcements are still a good idea.

The Honeymoon Wedding

Particularly appealing to workingwomen, the idea of a honeymoon wedding is simple: take a trip to a place you've always wanted to see, and get married. This kind of wedding is growing in popularity. The planning, however, might be complicated. Let's say you live on the East Coast and want to be married in Los Angeles. First find out what legal documents and physical tests are necessary for out-of-town residents. What identification will you need? Will a local blood test and license be accepted in California? It helps to have friends in Los Angeles researching this for you and making arrangements with an officiant to marry you, but if no friend or relative is available, you'll have to go through the excruciating and costly process of making long-distance inquiries to the marriage license bureau in Los Angeles. If you're lucky, you'll get the information quickly and without a lot of red tape. If you know an officiant or clergyman who will marry you, she or he can find out the specifics for you.

One romantic idea is to go all out and get married in Paris, London, or some other European city. Unfortunately, you can't be married in France unless you've lived there eight weeks—and you must be able to prove residency. The French government does not issue visas for the purpose of being married. If you are planning to live and work in France, you can obtain a visa, and residency can be established.

In England and Wales, you must file a petition with the church or civil authorities at least 7 days after entering the country, and then you have to wait a minimum of 3 weeks to a maximum of 3 months before getting married. The British Consulate in the United States will send you a form detailing the marriage requirements, but they don't encourage foreigners to plan weddings this way.

Most European countries have similar bureaucratic procedures which can be researched through a local consulate or the embassy in Washington, D.C. If special circumstances exist (e.g., your parents are living in Rome and you want to be married there), you may be able to obtain a special visa. Our State Department office of Citizen's Consular Services in Washington, D.C., can provide you with more detailed information regarding marrying abroad.

Guess what? Ship captains can't marry you. They have no legal authority to perform that ceremony. So planning a combination wedding-honeymoon cruise is difficult unless you take along your own clergyman or civil officiant. Some ocean liners do have chaplains aboard for long trips and can make arrangements for a marriage ceremony, but they don't encourage the idea, so don't get your hopes up.

Honeymoon weddings are a practical solution for couples whose professional lives are so complicated that planning a more traditional wedding and vacation trip is almost impossible. For people who travel a lot, an exotic business trip could be the incentive for a honeymoon wedding. Other couples simply reject the idea of marrying in their hometown because they want to avoid the additional work of making it perfect and the worry of who should be invited. Said one bride, "I was dreading the idea of planning a wedding—it was too much like what I do for a living. Instead, we took ten days to plan our out-of-town wedding and long-weekend honeymoon. It seems to me that people weren't nearly as hurt about not being invited as they would have been if we went off to City Hall."

The Long-distance Wedding

Marsha and Richard were living and working in Seattle, Washington, when they decided to get married. Their idea was to be married on Christmas Eve at the house of a close friend. About 20 people were invited to the wedding and cocktail reception that followed, and a judge they knew agreed to perform the ceremony. The problem was what to do about the families who were scattered in the Midwest, on the East Coast, and in the southern part of the country. Marsha and Richard agreed that asking their families to rearrange their Christmas holidays was unfair and impractical, and for most, the cost of a round-trip ticket to Seattle was prohibitive.

Their solution was to work with the telephone company to have conference phone systems installed in each of the five homes involved (this included her mother in Buffalo, New York; her father in New York City; her sister and family in Atlanta, Georgia; his father and mother in Chicago; and his sister in Boston). Each home had a special conference speaker box installed whereby a group of people could listen to the ceremony as it occurred in Seattle and speak back through the same sound system. (The standard hand receiver is not used, and voices can be picked up from as far away as eight or nine feet.) Naturally, the five sets of relatives were completely informed about the procedure, including the technical aspects, and each was asked to prepare a short toast or statement to be given at the end of the service.

The judge made sure that all five telephone lines were operating before the ceremony began, and when it was over, she called on each family to deliver a toast. Miraculously, it worked. All six homes (including the control house in Seattle) were received clearly and later reported hearing the ceremony and speeches without any problems. Marsha and Richard had the wit to tape-record the entire ceremony, and it was a joyful celebration, literally heard from coast to coast. At that time, in 1979, the cost for setting up the system for one day was five hundred dollars, or the price of one round-trip airline ticket from New York to Seattle.

Telephone companies offer this and other services through their business divisions. Their new PICTUREPHONE® Meeting Service, which provides live coverage of an event, is being developed now for national use.

It is probable that a number of weddings will be witnessed in full sound and color through this new technology, and the telephone company anticipates greater distribution of the system in the next few years.

If you want to arrange for a conference speakerphone system or PICTUREPHONE® Meeting Service, contact your local telephone business office at least 3 weeks before your wedding and outline your needs. You may, for example, want a portable conference telephone for more mobility at the ceremony site (average cost, about $25, with additional installation charges of about $45). Then, speakerphones can be installed in each city (average cost, about $15, with additional installation charges of about $45). It is possible that your local telephone company will arrange the entire system, but most likely each household will have to make separate arrangements.

From two weeks to one day before your wedding, dial "O" and ask to speak to the conference operator, who will arrange to place the calls at a given time on the day of your wedding. In addition to rental and installation costs for the equipment, you will have to pay the long-distance charges for each call. By the way, conference speakers can be installed in many major foreign cities. I wouldn't try to set it up on Easter Island, but Europe and Japan are pretty good bets.

Costs for renting PICTUREPHONE® Meeting Service rooms are available through the telephone company's business office. The room is set up with elaborate tape recording systems and video recording devices. At this time the system is not available for private homes or offices.

Home Sweet Weddings

Even if couples and their families can afford large, elaborate weddings, many prefer to get married at home. Because the average house, apartment, or loft has limited space and facilities, home weddings are usually more intimate and less formal than other styles. First, you'll need to decide where to get married. If you like your parents' house and they're willing to take the extra time and trouble to plan the wedding, go ahead. Or if you and your fiancé already share a space that can accommodate the number of guests you want to ask, you may host your own wedding. It's possible, too, that a close friend or relative will offer to host the wedding. This may be the best choice. As long as everyone understands whose wedding it is, there should be no problem.

Once you've chosen the space, you can estimate how many guests to ask, based on standing room. A living room, for example, that measures 25 by 14 feet and is not overly furnished would accommodate about 40 people, not including the bride, groom, officiant, and the special space they would occupy within that room. Home weddings can be set up formally or casually, depending on religious requirements and your personal taste.

The formal approach is to have an aisle, created by stanchions draped with ribbons or clusters of flowers, leading to the ceremony site. If the room is large enough, attractive folding chairs can be placed on either side of the aisle. If space is limited, seating should be available for older people who would be terribly uncomfortable otherwise. If you are not going to provide seats, make sure your families have the best standing room in the house.

A casual approach to the home wedding is equally acceptable. The bride—along with her fiancé—may or may not greet guests in advance of the ceremony. When all the guests have gathered, the officiant welcomes everyone to the joyous occasion, asks the bride and groom to step forward with their attendants (if they choose to have them), and the wedding takes place.

The ceremony itself is usually no different from the informal religious or standard civil service, and formal or informal, drinks are not served until the ceremony has ended. You don't want a chorus of clinking ice cubes as you say "I do." Music, on the other hand, is usually played while the guests gather. And a processional is appropriate for the more formal wedding. Home weddings can be held at any time of day or evening and can be followed by simple refreshments or a full-course meal. The house or apartment is usually decorated with flowers or potted plants, and if the wedding takes place in the evening, candles and lanterns can be carefully placed to supplement soft incandescent lighting. The bride can wear a wedding dress or a street-length dress or suit, but anything longer than a sweep train or fingertip veil would be obtrusive and unmanageable.

The groom can wear a business suit, a blazer and flannels, or, after six o'clock, a tuxedo. The bride can carry a small bouquet or nosegay; the groom, best man, and fathers might wear boutonnieres; mothers and grandmothers can have corsages. If this is a second wedding, any of your children could stand with you in their Sunday best.

I was recently involved with two lovely home weddings which illustrate some unique ideas and approaches. The first was held at a fabulous loft that was owned by friends of the bride and groom. The view of the urban landscape was breathtaking. The ceremony was scheduled for 2:00 P.M., and one hundred guests were invited. The bride's mother and groom's parents greeted people at the door and introduced them to the hosts, and a violinist provided the perfect background music for the simple Catholic ceremony that followed. The priest, groom, best man, matron of honor, and parents stood together on a raised platform in full view of everyone, and as the processional began, the bride, whose father was deceased, walked alone to the site. She wore a simple chiffon wedding dress and wreath of silk flowers. Before their final vows were taken, the couple recited passages from Yeats as a declaration of their love.

When the 20-minute ceremony ended, the catering staff went into action, passing champagne for the series of toasts that followed. A buffet of roast beef, rice salad, and vegetables was served after hot and cold hors d'oeuvres had been passed. A separate room had been set up for dancing, but rather than hire a band, the couple provided a disco sound system, and the sound technician made sure that the volume did not interfere with conversation in the main room.

Every detail—from the ceremony itself to the food and flower arrangements—had been carefully thought out. The result was a warm and intimate marriage ceremony followed by a sophisticated reception. As you can imagine, the party cost about $6,000 (or $60 per person).

The other wedding was equally successful, but a lot less expensive. Peter and Emily had been sharing an apartment for two years before their marriage. They wanted a small but elegant wedding, with no more than 50 guests. Their budget was $750. Since Emily liked to cook, she decided to prepare the food in advance for the buffet supper and hire two people to serve and clean up.

The ceremony was planned for 6:00 P.M., and a Protestant minister agreed to officiate. Although Emily and Peter broke tradition by hosting the wedding themselves, greeting guests together, and not hiring a caterer for the reception, they wanted a traditional ceremony. A best man and matron of honor were chosen to attend them, and the short ceremony was held by the fireplace. No one gave the bride away; there was no processional; and everyone knew in advance what the bride was wearing (a white silk damask street-length dress). Their parents weren't hosting or directly participating in this wedding, but Emily and Peter wanted to honor their mothers and fathers, so at the end of the service, Emily made a special toast to her parents for being supportive and loving throughout her life, and Peter brought tears to his father's eyes with his own words of thanks and love.

Rather than serve real champagne, they bought six bottles of French sparkling white wine at half the price. A self-service bar was set up, and plates, flatware, and glasses were rented for the occasion. With the exception of Emily's bouquet, the flowers consisted of begonia plants that Emily had grown from cuttings, and the pots were placed in wicker baskets for the table arrangement. The wedding cake was a gift from a friend who baked, iced, and decorated a two-tiered confection.

Peter took care of the music by taping a series of 90-minute cassettes. Chamber music was played before the ceremony, and a mixture of pop and rock was recorded for later. Following is an itemized list of what their wedding cost:

Fee to minister	$ 50
Bride's flowers	25
Bride's dress (can be worn again)	—
Groom's suit (already owned)	—
Bar, mixers, ice	200
Ragoût d'agneau White and wild rice Green salad Bread Hors d'oeuvres Cheese Pâté Crudités	200
Potting soil Wicker baskets	25
Two helpers	100

Tapes	16
Photos (Uncle John)	—
Rental of plates, glasses, flatware, cloth napkins, folding chairs	100
Total	$716

There are lots of styles for home weddings, and they can be as elaborate or uncomplicated as you want. A midmorning ceremony could be followed by a buffet brunch of croissants, quiche, and salad; and bloody marys, mimosas, and wine could take the place of highballs and champagne. And a cocktail reception is fine for a late-afternoon wedding. The idea is to open your home and your heart to the friends and relatives you've chosen to share your happiness.

The Garden Wedding

Weddings *alfresco* can be small and informal, large and elegant, or just plain comfortable and pretty. Since most yards or gardens are larger than any single room in the house, you can invite more people. But be careful. Unless you've arranged for a tent or canopy, the house will have to accommodate everyone if it rains.

Garden weddings are similar to home weddings but offer more choices because of the additional space. You can, for example, have a dance floor installed and hire a band for the occasion. If you like, you can have a larger wedding party with more bridesmaids and ushers. Long trains and veils are not practical, but picture hats and formal wedding attire can be worn. If space is no problem, you can probably have a sit-down dinner or buffet; or you can have an elegant picnic with cold meats, cheeses, breads, salads, and wine set up on picnic tables. (Incidentally, musicians—especially those with electronic instruments—will usually not agree to play without the protection of a tent or raised platform. And caterers feel the same way about protecting tables, chairs, barware, and linens.)

The ceremony site should be chosen for good visibility and acoustics. A pretty flowering tree or garden bed can be perfect, outlined with potted plants or stanchions draped with smilax or woven with daisies or rosebuds. You may want chairs set up on either side of an aisle for your immediate families. Otherwise, people usually stand during the ceremony. Remember that it is more difficult to hear in outdoor spaces, especially if there are street noises from cars, buses, or other vehicles. Consider amplifying the ceremony with a simple microphone and speaker system.

Garden weddings can be held at any hour, but if you want the ceremony at sunset and the reception after dark, you'll have to use spot and floodlights for the garden and special lights for the tents. Torches, gas lanterns, or candle lanterns can be used to light footpaths leading to the house or street. If you anticipate a parking problem near the house, you may want to hire someone who can provide valet parking. Also, it is a good idea to inform neighbors and even the local police department about the wedding, especially if the music and revelry will go on past midnight.

As beautiful as they are, garden weddings can be a lot of extra work. Lawns, flower beds, and shrubbery should be trimmed and made as attractive as possible. Said one bride wryly, "I always had a fantasy about the perfect outdoor wedding, but my childbearing years would be over before I could get the garden in shape." The house itself should be cleaned and ready to receive guests. Flower arrangements can be used to decorate the most exposed rooms in the house, and if a porch or deck is in view of the garden, baskets of hanging flowers (such as impatiens or begonias) look terrific. Porch and deck railings will look festive and beautiful draped with garlands of smilax or daisy chains.

If you're going to rent a tent (or canopy), be sure to measure the space you need from the stake points to the center. The large stakes are usually placed about twenty feet from the central vertical post, and when they're removed after the wedding, the remaining holes should be plugged and reseeded. If you plan on dancing, a separate floor has to be installed, for dancing on the lawn can ruin high-heeled silk shoes, that well-rehearsed two-step, and the grass itself. When the floor is removed, it is possible that brown patches will appear on the lawn. They should disappear with proper aeration and watering, but you may want to ask a gardener or nursery expert how to prevent fungus or disease.

The ceremony at a garden wedding is handled similarly to a home wedding service. For an informal religious or civil ceremony, the officiant, the bride's father, or the best man will ask guests to gather near

Home and Garden Weddings

Ceremony Options	For 0–50 Guests	For 50–75	For 75 or More
Processional	Optional, but attendants are not included. You may enter with any relative you wish, with your fiancé, or alone	Optional, but it helps get everyone's attention	Optional, but a good idea, since people will expect a formal entrance
Attendants	One maid or matron of honor, one best man (include your kids, if you have any)	Up to two each, your children, or one special child attendant	As many as you like
Formal altar setting (in accordance with religious tradition)	Nothing, or perhaps simple candles or flower arrangement	Optional	Good idea
Wedding clothes	Floor-length dress with simple hat or short veil; or street-length dress or suit with hat, hair flowers, or face veil Business suit; blazer and flannels; tuxedo for evening Attendants may make their own choices	Bride may also want sweep train and floor-length veil Groom can wear morning suit (stroller) or cutaway Coordinated clothing for attendants is optional	Formal or informal, but long trains and veils could be cumbersome The groom can wear cutaway for afternoon wedding Coordinated clothing good for more than three attendants
Receiving line	Not necessary	Optional	Good idea
Reception choices	Cake and champagne, breakfast, brunch, lunch, cocktails and hors d'oeuvres, full-course buffet or sit-down dinner	Same	Cake and champagne alone is not substantial enough

the site. If music is available, a processional can signal the bride's entrance. For formal weddings, an aisle is cordoned off, the processional begins (usually played by a chamber music quartet, a pianist, or an organist), and the ceremony takes place. Again, there is no recessional, but a receiving line can be formed to greet guests.

Home and Garden Wedding Footnotes

You probably already know how formal or traditional you want your wedding to be, but some choices are affected by the number of people invited, the time of the wedding, and the size and formality of the house or garden. The following illustration provides some guidelines to help you in your planning. Across the board, it's your choice.

The Traditional Wedding

Here's a familiar story. Anne and David were not exactly a traditional couple. They lived together for two years before their marriage, attended more est meetings than Sunday church services, would travel up to 250 miles to hear the latest new wave rock group, and dressed in the funkiest, punkiest clothes they could find. Their landlord thought them pleasant, though odd. The grocer was baffled by their interest in whether the packaged vegetables were organically grown. And friends were delighted by their trendy discoveries and devil-may-care attitudes. You'd expect people like Anne and David to be married on top of a mountain by the guru of their choice, followed by a reception of herbal teas and macrobiotic food. Wrong.

In a shocking reversal, Anne and David got married in church in a traditional Protestant ceremony that included a long walk down the aisle. "I don't think it was out of character for David and me to want our wedding to be more serious than an evening out at the roller disco," explained Anne. "Besides, when you get married, you kind of want God on your side, too."

For the record, almost 65 percent of all weddings are traditional. And even though they range from informal to superformal, they are always held in a church or temple, are characterized by solemn religious vows, and are witnessed by the community. As such, traditional wedding ceremonies—including the more contemporary and personal services—are often the most awe-inspiring, representing the past and the future in a beautiful way.

If your religious affiliations are tenuous, at best, and you like the idea of being married in the church or temple of your childhood, you and your parents could probably square it with the clergyman, as long as you agree to sit through a serious lecture regarding your spiritual salvation. If going home to be married is not practical, you can make arrangements locally. Be prepared, however, to explain why you are not a member of the congregation, why you want to be married there, etc.

Although you may decide to choose a less formal style, here's your chance to wear a wedding dress with a long train or veil. If you're dressing up, the groom should, too, and the pageant of bridesmaids, ushers, flower girls, and ring bearers should be coordinated to the size and style of the wedding.

Large churches usually have smaller chapels which are appropriate for intimate and less formal weddings. All decisions concerning the type of ceremony, the legal and religious requirements, and the music, photography, tapes, films, rice, confetti, receiving lines, and decorations can be made in consultation with the clergyman. It is customary for most churches and temples to ask you to complete a questionnaire regarding your marital status and your religious beliefs, and to give a brief personal history.

Church fees vary, but to give you an idea, St. Patrick's Cathedral in New York asks $200 for the use of the church (which seats 2,500 people), $150 for the chapel (which seats 100), $35 for the soloist, and $60 for the organist. This does not include an honorarium for the clergyman, which is usually no less than the fee for the organist. In some cases, no fees are required, but a donation to the church, along with separate gratuities for the clergyman, the sexton, et al. are "appreciated." In situations of extreme poverty, most fees are waived.

If you are planning a church wedding on the third Saturday in June, it's wise to make your reservations early. Find out, too, if any other weddings are planned for that day and if there is a potential conflict in timing.

How to Handle the Clergy

Despite the fact that most clerics will want to cooperate with you on your choices for the ceremony, there are reports that some clergymen don't honestly know the difference between their own tastes and prejudices and the laws of the church. They may say, for example, that no one other than the official church organist can play at your wedding. Or that "O Promise Me" has to be sung. Or that you and your groom can't walk down the aisle together. Or that you may not, under any circumstances, write your own vows or otherwise speak to each other without repeating after him.

You have three choices: (1) accept his dictates and relinquish all prerogatives, (2) persuade him to consider and accept your reasonable ideas, or (3) find another cleric who can perform the ceremony with you in mind. Remember that there may be real reasons to support certain rules. If a Greek Orthodox priest asks you not to wear a wide-brimmed hat, it is because a crown must be placed on your head during the ceremony. He may, however, agree to have you remove the hat and hand it to your attendant.

Don't be afraid to discuss your ideas openly and honestly. If you're not making any progress, get a second opinion by asking a higher authority in the church to consider your requests. Just remember that you're dealing with a representative of your church or synagogue, not a merchant.

Thoughts for the Second Time Around

In the old days, remarriage was considered an overt act of rudeness, and couples were advised by etiquette experts to keep a low profile. The list of don'ts was always longer than the dos, and wearing a white dress or having attendants, large receptions, or anything that remotely resembled a virginal formal wedding was strictly taboo. But now, with more than 720,000 remarriages a year, the rules have changed to allow all brides the same choices. Some faiths will not permit divorced people to marry again without a church annulment or its equivalent, and many clerics will discourage you from trying to have a traditional wedding under any circumstances. Still, if your religion is no obstacle to a formal wedding, neither is modern etiquette. If you eloped the first time and want to make up for it now with a big wedding, go ahead. Just don't expect your parents to pay.

Most second weddings do tend to be intimate celebrations rather than grand spectacles—and this is because the couple prefers it. The one thing you want, this time, is to look and act like the woman you are. This means (a) wearing a dress that reflects your personal style, (b) not playing the demure little girl whose life is just beginning, (c) probably not letting Dad give you away again, and (d) hosting a reception that fits your ideas of entertaining.

If either of you has children, the marriage symbolically unites the families as well as the husband and wife. As such, the kids should have a special place in the wedding. The trend is toward having the kids participate as witnesses or attendants, usually in lieu of other people. If you're walking down the aisle, your kids could precede you, or you can march with them. His children would flank him at the altar.

During the ceremony, the clergyman might want to include a special acknowledgment of the children, or you might want to say something that makes them feel important. Older children may be able to contribute to the ceremony by reciting an appropriate prayer or poem.

On the other hand, if children are ambivalent or even angry about the marriage, they should not be forced to participate in the ceremony. Well in advance of the wedding, you should try to help them express their feelings and to understand yours. It is one way of getting your remarriage off to a good start.

Military Fanfare

Years ago, when Hollywood was making movies about West Point or Annapolis, military weddings were fashionable endings to four years of officer training in our special academies. Then came Vietnam, the end of the draft, and sometimes undeserved criticism of anything or anyone even remotely connected with the military establishment. For some people, the drawn swords that create an arch of steel at the end of the ceremony are symbols of war and aggression and, as such, have no place at a wedding or a house of God.

If you have no problem separating church and state, and if you or your groom and the ushers are commissioned officers, you may want to have what has come to be known as a military wedding. Actually, this is a misnomer. There is no such thing as a military wedding. There is simply a military ending to a formal church service. After the ceremony, either at the chancel steps or outside the church (depending on what's allowed by the faith), at least four ushers in full military dress face each other. On command by the head usher, they will either arch their sabers (army) or draw their swords (navy), with the cutting blades on top. Only the bride and groom pass under the arch, and when the swords are sheathed, the ushers pair up with the bridesmaids and leave the church. This ritual started in 1909 when the groom and groomsmen took to raising their sabers to toast the bride. The idea was later formalized and became accepted as military tradition.

Military protocol overrides some wedding etiquette, especially as it applies to uniforms and invitations (forms of address). To find answers to specific questions or problems, protocol officers or hostesses are available at military academies or on military bases.

For the record, the military ceremony is available to any officer—including women. Female ushers can raise swords and sabers. And an officer-bride, even if she chooses to marry a civilian and wear a white dress, is eligible for the ceremony.

The Double Wedding

I suppose there are some situations that justify double weddings, but I get an eerie feeling about Bob and Carol and Ted and Alice when I think about four adults sharing their very individual wedding vows. If sisters are involved and the guest list is similar, it probably makes sense to double up, but you may consider having smaller private ceremonies and a joint reception later on.

For a formal double ceremony, each couple can have their own attendants, or the brides and grooms can be maid and matron of honor and best men for each other. Double weddings don't work if you're sensitive about your age because, traditionally, the older bride goes first at the processional, the ceremony, and the recessional. Here again, however, there are choices: sisters can be escorted together by their father; the two couples can walk down the left and right aisles simultaneously; or one couple can be first at the processional, the other at the recessional.

5 · Telling People the News

"What bothered me most," said Marilyn when she heard about the wedding plans of a friend, "was that Clara went around flashing her diamond ring and pretending that her coming marriage was the result of an old-fashioned courtship. Not only had she and Mitch lived together for two years, but she had a hell of a time convincing him to make it legal. All of a sudden, Clara became a born-again virgin!"

Clara wasn't really out to falsify her status or one-up her friends. She was simply trying to meet people's expectations by acting "properly engaged" whenever she broke the news. Clara probably took her cues from the late-night movies.

Even though most women feel great joy about getting married, many hesitate to show their happiness publicly. If you've been living together, an engagement might seem anticlimactic. Or you may feel guilty about betraying those early ideals of remaining independent from the legal trap of marriage. Or you may still be suffering a hangover from the days when marriage just wasn't "in." And so, rather than joyously announcing your wedding intentions, you meekly and defensively say you're only getting married because you want to avoid those reproachful glances from your superintendent.

In one of his columns for the *New York Times,* Russell Baker once said that people are getting married again because they don't know what label to use to describe their relationship. His fictional couple, Tess and Pietro, tried everything from "This is my mate" to "This is the man in my life." Baker tells the story: "As Tess explained at the wedding, they couldn't spend the rest of their lives rolling their eyeballs suggestively every time they said, 'friend.' There was only one way out. 'The simple thing,' Pietro suggested, 'would be for me to introduce you as "my wife." ' 'And for me,' said Tess, 'to say, "This is my husband, Pietro." ' And so they were married, victims of a failure in English."

The most important thing is not to be defensive about getting married. If people have the bad taste and judgment to challenge your decision, don't get embroiled in explaining why you're doing it. If they offer good cheer and congratulations, accept gracefully without discussing how you were both finally ready to make this kind of commitment. Most people will not only be happy for you, they'll offer help and advice, some of which can be useful. Announcing your wedding plans should never be done by shouting, nor should it be done in a whisper. The way you tell people your plans will to some extent control their reactions, and those reactions will not always be what you expect.

Telling Your Parents

If your parents live out of town, call them. If they know your fiancé, he should speak with them, too. If they haven't met him, say that the two of you plan to visit them soon. By the way, it's a nice gesture for you and your fiancé to visit parents at their homes. This is a courtesy and a tradition that most couples follow, unless financial circumstances prevent them from making a costly trip. Old etiquette requires his parents to call yours and plan a visit, if possible, but some couples prefer to host a dinner themselves so that the respective parents can meet. None of this is absolutely necessary, but most people agree that it is a good idea for all to get acquainted in advance of the wedding, especially if the costs are to be shared. If your parents are divorced, you should proceed to contact them separately, offering each the same courtesy of meeting your fiancé and his family. Your good judgment will help you decide how or even if to approach a divorced parent whom you haven't seen in years.

Remember, if at this point you don't know what kind of wedding you want, your mother is apt to take over. You can temper her energetic planning by telling her that you'll discuss the details when you see her.

Some parents will flatly disapprove of your fiancé and will try to discourage you from marrying. They may have strict religious ideas;

they may think he's not successful enough; or they may simply be disappointed that you didn't marry the doctor next door. If they react in this way, make it clear that your decision is final and that you hope they'll change their minds. But don't get into a telephone battle or armed combat at the dinner table. Unless your parents have concrete evidence that your intended is a secret ax murderer, they shouldn't try to prevent the marriage.

Telling the Children

If either you or he has children from a former marriage, they should be told first. This is a toughie. No matter how well you get along with the kids, they're apt to feel conflicted about the marriage. Young children often have fantasies about their parents getting back together, and a new marriage threatens that concept, but children also know that it's not so bad to have an alternative mother or father who can act as another role model.

What kids really want is some stability in their lives, and a new parent can provide it. Without feeling guilty or tentative, the two of you should sit down with the kids, possibly over the dinner table, and tell them how happy you are about getting married and how you hope they'll be happy about it, too. Karen and Kristin, ten- and twelve-year-old sisters whose parents have both married again, have suggested that parents tell their kids and celebrate with them. "I think there should be a cake or an ice-cream sundae to make it official," said Karen.

An ice-cream sundae, however, can't cover up the fear and anger that might emerge at this time. Kristin's father said that his daughter sobbed uncontrollably when he told her the news. After she calmed down, she explained that she was afraid that if he married, he would get divorced and she'd never see Betty (the parent-to-be) again. Kristin was reassured by both Betty and her father that they would always be part of her life. They also knew that Kristin wanted to talk more about the divorce and why it happened. The result was a meaningful discussion which helped Kristin understand that even though her real parents didn't love each other anymore, they both loved her and always would.

Other kids, in an effort to get Daddy's or Mommy's attention away from the parent-to-be, will behave destructively or rebelliously.

What's needed is a lot of reassurance that the child's parent won't love him or her less because of the new marriage.

After learning about the marriage plans, a child might withdraw, building a protective shell against another unsettling change. Give him plenty of time to get used to the idea, and help to draw him out so that he can express his feelings. If you think the problem is beyond your control, consider contacting a family counseling service or child psychologist.

Your fiancé's older children, especially teen-agers, might surprise you by saying that they want to live with you, or, if you have children of your own, by saying that they want to leave you for their father. Young adolescents are just beginning to realize that they can control their world by making their own choices. These children are either testing you by asking, Do you love me enough to have me live with you? or rejecting you because they feel you've rejected them in favor of the new spouse.

In movie fantasies, the child encourages the single parent to remarry and becomes supportive and understanding. If you get that kind of response from a teen-age son or daughter, consider yourself lucky and don't look for trouble where none exists. As always, a good healthy dialogue should be created to air feelings and help children understand that there are no limits on how much one person can love.

No matter what their age, kids should be included in the wedding. Older children can be witnesses, younger ones flower girls or ring bearers. If the/ have no specific function, kids should stand with their parents and have an opportunity to participate in the wedding. If there are special problems between the child and the future stepparent or if the child is still suffering an extreme case of divorce shock, don't insist that she or he take part in the wedding, and try to help this child work out her or his feelings before you get married.

Most little kids want to go with you on your honeymoon (if you have one). They don't understand why you're going away, and they might be afraid that you won't come back. First of all, *don't* take them along; you can plan your family outings later. But do explain that this is a special trip for the two of you—that it's traditional, and that you'll send them funny postcards or call them from your hotel.

If the children live with you most of the time, they're apt to experience the kind of separation anxiety that can occur with any trip you might make. Ideally, the other parent will take over during this time, but if he or she is unable to, a grandmother or other close relative is your next best choice.

Telling Your Friends

Sociologists present the theory that when two people marry, the friends and relatives that surrounded one person's life are reevaluated through the eyes of the other. It's as if married people create a third perception of their world and the people in it. For many couples, this perception can alter relationships, limiting or eliminating some and encouraging others. Sometimes friends themselves make the decision by accepting or rejecting the new spouse. In any case, being sensitive and aware of the feelings of your friends is crucial to helping them understand your new life.

In *The Way of All Flesh,* Samuel Butler wrote, "A man's friendships are, like his will, invalidated by marriage, but they are also no less invalidated by the marriage of his friends." The message here is that your friendships will be changed by your marriage. Close friends might feel threatened about losing you as an ally in the single life.

Don't be surprised or offended if some friends start to withdraw from you at this time. If they've been particularly dependent on you for their social life, they might attach themselves to a new person who can "go out and play" at the drop of a hat. But after an initial period of withdrawal or tension, your friends will probably "return," with a new insight into your relationship. Don't expect your fiancé to love your friends, and vice versa. If it happens, fine, but playing matchmaker between friends and lovers can be a fruitless endeavor.

If you plan to announce your marriage plans to a large group of friends, there are a lot of creative ways of doing it. One romantic woman had planned a surprise birthday party for her man, to be held at an elegant restaurant. He found out, hired a limousine, stocked it with champagne, and presented her with his family's heirloom jewelry as well as an old-fashioned down-on-the-knees marriage proposal. She said yes, and the birthday party became a double celebration.

Another couple thought the opening day of their summer softball game would be the perfect opportunity to announce their plans. They brought hot dogs and hamburgers and a case of champagne, and they kicked off the season with a picnic-cum-engagement party. It didn't matter that all the weekend athletes were grubby and achy from the season's first effort. The important thing was to gather a community of friends to share in the good news.

By the way, it is best not to announce your plans at someone else's wedding. It's not fair to turn attention away from the bride and groom.

Telling Out-of-towners

If Uncle Charlie from Terre Haute was always one of your favorites, call him yourself to tell him the news. Otherwise, let your parents break the news to the rest of the family and friends of theirs from out of town. As far as your friends are concerned, you may certainly call or write, but if you haven't seen them for a while, don't let your wedding plans dominate the conversation. Find out what's new in their lives, too. Some of these friends will expect to be invited to the wedding and will travel to be there. Others won't be able to. Don't pressure them to make the trip. They might resent being made to feel guilty.

Telling the People at Work

An ambitious friend of mine came up with an inventive approach to telling her boss about her marriage plans. She simply asked for a hefty raise to help support her new life-style, thereby making it clear that she had no intention of abandoning her career because of her marriage. Her boss must have realized that she expected to be given new opportunities to rise in the organization, for she received a 15-percent increase on her annual salary and approval of the two-week vacation she wanted.

Women who feel strongly about separating their personal and professional lives might never mention their wedding plans to their bosses, preferring instead to let the grapevine speak for them. But women who enjoy a team spirit at work often make a special effort to introduce their fiancés to their co-workers and bosses.

For men in business, marriage means a pat on the back and a "welcome, my boy, to the club." For professional women, marriage can jeopardize their careers. No matter how much we want to believe that discrimination is a thing of the past, we must be realistic about the corporate reaction to marriage, pregnancy, or other nesting symbols, such as the acquisition of a dog or a mongoose. One female executive expressed her feelings: "When a woman gets married in this department, her work suffers. Lunch hours are extended to meet with caterers; the telephone is alive with calls from mothers; and secretaries are asked to type up guest lists rather than the latest annual report. Maybe I'm exaggerating, but I honestly feel that when a woman plans a wedding, she takes her job less seriously."

What a lot of people don't realize is that the reverse is often true. When your personal life is in order, you're going to concentrate even more on your career. One bride put it this way: "Marriage gave me the stability I wanted in my private life. I stopped worrying about dating and started to think about new ways to cut production costs."

This is a good time to keep a low profile at the office. It's okay to make some personal calls at appropriate times, but don't discuss the results of your research or offer a play-by-play account of how things are going. If you have a secretary, don't assume that she or he will be willing to help you with the wedding any more than she or he would jump at the chance to get your coffee. If a secretary offers to help, lucky you. If not, and you really need help, offer to pay for their services, rendered after working hours.

Obviously, if you have no personal ties to the people you work with, it is not necessary to tell them anything.

Telling Ex-wives and Ex-husbands

If you are friendly with an ex-spouse, call or write. Otherwise, you have no obligation to tell them your plans. No matter what, an ex is not invited to the wedding; that only happens in fiction.

6 • The Announcement

Some couples want a year or so to plan a wedding, find a diamond ring, and star in a series of prewedding parties. They might want to announce their plans in the newspaper or make a formal statement to family and friends at a special party. Others might prefer to minimize the prewedding hoopla, especially if they're marrying for the second time or have been living together. But whether you consider yourselves "engaged" or not, you can choose to go along with some of the traditions and reject others.

Newspaper Announcements

Traditionally, a newspaper engagement announcement is issued by the bride's parents and includes pertinent information about the couple's education and their careers, as well as background on the parents' professional achievements. When giving information, be as specific as possible about job titles and degrees. Don't say that your father works for Standard Oil; say he's vice-president in charge of distribution. Avoid nicknames and abbreviations, and be sure to include any special information, such as the fact that George Washington was your great-great-great-grandfather. According to Woodene Merriman, an editor at the *Pittsburgh Post Gazette,* the most commonly made mistakes are not typing the information and not including the full names of the man's parents. The *Gazette* has simplified engagement announcements by printing concisely worded notices in small-type column form. With regard to wedding announcements, said Ms. Merriman, the greatest error people make is sending them in too late:

"If we don't receive an announcement within two weeks of the wedding, it probably won't run."

Don't be surprised if your local newspaper charges a fee for printing engagement and wedding announcements. The *Washington Post* initiated this policy a number of years ago in order to accommodate the large volume of requests. Prior to that, cryptic little notices would appear without photographs or background information, and even then, a lot of people were left out. The *Post* charges $28 per column inch of space or $4 per single-column printed line. By measuring a few announcements, you can determine how much they would cost. Don't forget to include the space for the photograph.

The following is an example of how you might word your engagement notice:

> Mr. and Mrs. John Doe of Atlanta, Ga., announce the engagement of their daughter, Miss Patricia Morris Doe, to Mr. Robert Aldrich Peters, son of Mr. and Mrs. Charles Peters of Columbus, Ohio. A May wedding is planned.
>
> Miss Doe, an alumna of Swarthmore College, received a master's degree from the Harvard Business School. She is with the marketing division of Eastman-Kodak Company. Her father is the chairman of the board of Polaroid Corporation.
>
> Mr. Peters was graduated from Williams College and the Columbia Graduate School of Business. He is a vice-president of Xerox Corporation. His mother served as a United States representative from Ohio.

If you want to announce your engagement yourselves, your parents' names would be included as follows:

> Patricia Morris Doe, a marketing executive of Eastman-Kodak Company, plans to be married in May to Robert Aldrich Peters, a vice-president of the Xerox Corporation.
>
> Miss Doe, daughter of Mr. and Mrs. John Doe of Atlanta, Ga., was graduated from Swarthmore College and received a master's degree from the Harvard Business School.
>
> Mr. Peters, a graduate of Williams College and the Columbia Graduate School of Business, is the son of Mr. and Mrs. Charles Peters of Columbus, Ohio. His mother served as a United States representative from Ohio.

Since newspapers have limited space, they're apt to edit the information you provide. Some, for example, will not use the glossy photograph you send. Others will cut what they consider to be unimportant information about yourselves or your parents. Still others, such as the *New York Times,* might not run the item at all. Because space is so limited in a large metropolitan daily, whether or not your announcement runs might depend on how professionally or socially prominent you or your families are. It is a good idea to call the society editor of your local newspaper before preparing the announcement. Some will send you a form to fill out, and others will request a typewritten release. You may, of course, send the same announcement to more than one newspaper. You might want your parents to announce the engagement in their hometown as well as your fiancé's. (His parents do not make an announcement.) You can then send out your own release to newspapers in the place where you live and work. If parents are deceased, divorced, or remarried, the wording changes.

If one parent is deceased, the announcement should read as follows:

> Mrs. (or Mr.) John Doe of Atlanta, Ga., announces the engagement of her (his) daughter, Miss Patricia Morris Doe, to Mr. Robert Aldrich Peters, son of Mr. and Mrs. Charles Peters of Columbus, Ohio. Miss Doe is also the daughter of the late John Doe.

If your parents are divorced, it should read:

> Mrs. (or Mr.) John Doe of Atlanta, Ga., announces the engagement of her (his) daughter, Miss Patricia Morris Doe, to Mr. Robert Aldrich Peters, son of Mr. and Mrs. Charles Peters of Columbus, Ohio. Miss Doe is also the daughter of Mr. John Doe.

If one parent is remarried:

> Mr. and Mrs. Alan Smith of Atlanta, Ga., announce the engagement of Mrs. Smith's daughter, Miss Patricia Morris Doe, to Mr. Robert Aldrich Peters, son of Mr. and Mrs. Charles Peters of Columbus, Ohio. Miss Doe is also the daughter of Mr. John Doe of Tulsa, Oklahoma.

If your parents are divorced amicably:

> Mrs. Alan Smith of Atlanta, Ga., and Mr. John Doe of Tulsa, Oklahoma, announce the engagement of their daughter, Miss Patricia Morris Doe, to Mr. Robert Aldrich Peters. . . .

With some exceptions, newspapers still follow traditional etiquette for engagement and wedding announcements, but some of the criteria have changed. According to a society editor at the *New York Times,* there is currently less emphasis on when or whether you made your debut and more attention paid to your career and professional achievements, as well as those of your mother. Also, more space is being devoted to couples marrying for the second or third time.

Other Announcements

Some magazines, in an effort to encourage community involvement, are running personal announcements of births, deaths, and marriages. These are not society columns, per se, as much as a community bulletin board service. One- or two-line announcements in very small type are the extent of the editorial service, and you may want to be included. Otherwise, couples can pay for a personal ad in the classified section.

If you want the graduating class of 1970 to know about your marriage, send an item to your alumni journal. Most have a personal column, and they're usually desperate to fill it.

You may also want to make an announcement in your firm's newspaper. You can phone in the information. It may not beat the old-fashioned grapevine in getting the word around, but it is an efficient way of breaking the news at work.

Announcement Parties

A lot of people love a good excuse to give a party, and a wedding is the ultimate trigger situation. Your parents, for example, might plan to make a formal announcement at a cocktail reception or dinner dance in your honor. If you hate the idea, discourage them. If it fits the budget and you think it would be fun, go ahead and enjoy every minute of it. There is one rule that applies to most prewedding parties: unless your wedding will be a small, intimate celebration, be sure that anyone invited to these parties is also on the wedding guest list.

The formal dinner dance is a gala affair and it's expensive. (I have a hunch that the idea became popular because of a Grace Kelly movie.) Unless your parents' house is grand enough to have a separate ballroom, this kind of party is held at a club or hotel. You need enough people to fill the dance floor, a band, a staff of waiters and chefs that can handle a five-course meal, and a father who's still sober enough to make an elegant toast to the happy couple. There is usually a glittering array of the latest evening dresses, and men generally don tuxedoes. Obviously, if you do this for an engagement, you'll want to top it at the wedding.

The buffet dinner, for a smaller group of people, is still a pretty formal way of announcing an engagement. Again, clubs, hotels, or spacious private houses can be used. You don't need a band, but you should have some music. A pianist, chamber music quartet, or classical guitarist is appropriate.

The cocktail reception is easier for several reasons. First, there's a time limit. Cocktail parties usually start at six or seven in the evening and end by nine. Second, they're less costly. Hot and cold hors d'oeuvres are passed, and one round of champagne is all that's necessary for purposes of the announcement. Music is still a good idea, but you can use a tape system rather than live entertainment. In addition to clubs, hotels, and houses, you can use apartments, lofts, restaurants with private reception facilities, and yachts.

Teas and ladies' luncheons are no longer very popular because few workingwomen have time to spend long hours socializing in the afternoon. If your women friends fit this profile, don't plan a girls' day out.

Picnics, barbecues, barn dances, clambakes, and weekend brunches can all be fun and appropriate for the occasion. In most parts of the country, the cheese and wine party has been discovered and dismissed.

Any close friend or relative can give a party in your honor, but no one should be expected to. In today's economy, parties are apt to be hosted jointly by a group of friends or relatives. For some, it's a creative wedding gift, and you should expect no more. People don't usually give engagement gifts, but if they do, write a prompt thank-you note.

Rings and Other Things

In 1477, Maximilian I of Austria gave Mary of Burgundy a big fat diamond ring to seal their engagement. Max and Mary probably didn't know that they started a brand-new tradition that many couples take very seriously, but for all the reasons that Mary of Burgundy and Elizabeth Taylor are comfortable with diamonds, you may not be. Here's the point: you are no less engaged without a diamond ring. If you like the tradition and can afford a ring, earrings, or anything else, fine. But if you prefer to spend the money on an antique Tiffany lamp, do it. And if you don't want to spend the money at all, don't.

Modern-day Etiquette

Old etiquette guides sternly caution couples against going off without a chaperone. The problem couples face today is whether to tell their parents they've been living together.

It is almost impossible to come up with a consensus. If parents are sophisticated and avant-garde, it might be no problem. If, however, they believe that this is yet another example of how the country is heading for a downfall, think again.

Most couples agree that the less said, the better, but that you shouldn't lie if asked. Others think that a lot of parents really know the truth but don't want to confront their kids or admit it to themselves. At one couple's wedding, a good friend and very funny man stood up to propose a toast. Everyone laughed when he lovingly alluded to their prenuptial living arrangements. Everyone except the bride's mother, father, grandmother, and great-aunt. It was a credit to them that they never did bring it up with their daughter, but this was no way to find out.

It's unlikely that your mother will take you aside at this time to explain the facts of life. But if Grandma chooses to lecture you about the marriage bed, don't try to enlighten her with findings from Masters and Johnson. Good judgment counts.

How to Call It Off

Here's an interesting statistic: people who have "quickie" weddings are more likely to get divorced than those who take time for planning. The reason: if you are going to change your mind, you will have time to do it during the so-called engagement. Said Shakespeare, a "hasty marriage seldom proveth well."

If you are convinced that your imminent marriage will be a big mistake, don't go ahead with it just because you've already received some wedding gifts or because you don't want to disappoint your family. It's your life, after all, and you have every right to delay the wedding or cancel it entirely.

You should, of course, return any gifts (such as a ring) given to you by your fiancé. If wedding invitations have not been sent, people can be notified casually by phone or letter that the marriage won't take place. If the invitations have been mailed, send a formal engraved note explaining that the wedding will not take place or that it is being postponed. Otherwise, telegrams and phone calls are the best way. When you return a gift to someone, send a note saying, "I'm sorry to tell you that Bob and I have broken our engagement (or will not be getting married). Your very thoughtful gift is being mailed to you separately. I hope to see you soon."

If you do decide to call it off, go see *The Philadelphia Story* and study Katharine Hepburn's wonderful wit, grace, and style. Even if the story didn't end happily, she never would have played the role of a simpering soap opera maiden. And neither should you. Don't offer lengthy explanations or horrible details of his behavior.

7 · The Ceremony

At the heart of the marriage ceremony is a solemn contract. Though some people treat a wedding as a bit of theater in which they can star, the real purpose is a public exchange of vows. Both parties commit themselves to stay together, even if one loses a job or a leg, gains 50 pounds, or plunges into mid-life crisis. Obviously you can't predict the future, or how things might change during the course of your marriage, but you should be truly conscious of every word you say at the ceremony. If traditional vows are unacceptable, you can usually edit or change them, as long as you don't disregard the laws of your faith or the state.

In response to the demand from couples to modify and personalize the wedding service, religious institutions have done their share to update the ceremony, at the same time preserving those aspects that are integral to the laws of their respective faiths. You must remember that most traditional churches and synagogues discourage having their rituals watered down. Still, although some members of the clergy were horrified by the freewheeling weddings of the sixties, many churches have made reforms and do allow couples to adapt part of the ceremony.

Because they no longer go to church or synagogue on a regular basis, a lot of people who would prefer a religious ceremony to a civil service are afraid to approach the clergy. Many couples assume that they'll have no clout to negotiate their wedding service, so the idea of a religious ceremony is dropped altogether. Others feel hypocritical about "using their religion" as a convenience. This is too bad, since most religious establishments welcome any sign of renewed faith, even if the couple are strangers or are ambivalent about other aspects of their faith.

It is true that clergymen are not required to marry anyone, but most won't refuse if they are convinced that the couple has serious intentions to live up to the commitment of marriage. If you want to strike out every reference to fidelity, love, and God, the clergy will probably wonder why you want to get married in the first place, let alone in a place of worship. In short, if you want marriage solely on your terms, don't expect religious approval.

The Catholic Ceremony

The Catholic marriage ceremony is one of seven sacraments that the church acknowledges as signs of God's grace. As such, it is essential that a priest administer the sacrament by presiding at the marriage service. At minimum, the ceremony consists of three readings (one from the Old Testament, one from the New Testament, and one from the Gospels), the marriage rite itself, the nuptial blessing, and the concluding prayers. The ceremony is, however, often held within the context of a mass, where the couple themselves and other Catholics may receive the Sacrament of Holy Communion.

The Catholic church encourages a couple's participation in the wedding service and has made available a number of choices of hymns, prayers, and readings. Although some priests and parishes will not allow the marriage rite to be changed, others will. You should discuss all these options with your priest in order to determine how traditional or contemporary you want your wedding to be.

Most of the priests I spoke with observe a marked trend back to the traditional Catholic wedding service. To their surprise, many couples are not interested in completely renovating the classic ritual. For example, one couple, Debra and Kevin, modified only those aspects of the traditional service that conflicted with their lives. Kevin is Catholic and Debra is Baptist. The officiating priest was a friend of the bride's, and the ceremony was held at a Catholic church in her hometown. There was no nuptial mass. After the processional, the priest welcomed family and friends and offered a brief prayer. This was followed by the liturgy of the word (the three readings). The first, from the Old Testament, was read by one of Debra's bridesmaids The second, from the New Testament, was read by Kevin's father. (Traditionally, these are read by the priest.) The third reading from the Gospels was recited by the priest.

The priest then offered a homily—or brief sermon—on the meaning of marriage; it was tailored to his knowledge of the two individuals and their families. At this wedding, the homily ended with a quote from a Robert Frost poem.

The rite of marriage was next (unchanged from the traditional vows), followed by the blessings and the exchange of rings. Kevin and Debra chose to include the optional candle ceremony—the lighting of a single candle to symbolize their marital unity. The priest then offered the Prayer of the Faithful. The Prayer of the Couple was next, and for this the church allows people to create their own prayer or change the recommended reading. Kevin and Debra changed the reading as follows. The words in parentheses were deleted. The phrase in italics was added.

> *Kevin and Debra:* Our Father in heaven, we now stand before you and we are very happy (but somewhat nervous). You brought us together in the beginning, helped our love grow, and at this moment are with us in a special way. We ask that you stay by our side in the days ahead. Protect us from anything which might harm our marriage, give us courage when burdens come our way, teach us to forgive one another when we fail.
>
> *Kevin:* I ask from you assistance to be a good husband (and father). Never let me take my wife for granted or forget she needs to be loved. (If you bless us with children, I promise to love them, to care for them, to give them the best possible example.)
>
> *Debra:* I ask your assistance to be a good wife (and mother). (May I never forget how important my husband's work is for his happiness or fail to give him encouragement. If you bless me with motherhood, I promise to give myself totally to the children, even to the point of stepping aside when they must walk alone.) *Help us to support each other as individuals and in our careers. Never let us forget that our marriage comes first.*
>
> *Kevin and Debra:* We ask, finally, that in our old age we may love one another as deeply and cherish each other as much as we do at this very moment. May you grant these wishes which we offer through your son, Jesus Christ our Lord.

As you can see, Kevin and Debra did not want to commit themselves to having children. And Debra, who did not convert to Catholicism, was leery of promising to raise children in the Catholic faith. It is required that the Catholic partner make a promise, either in writing or orally, that states, "I reaffirm my faith in Jesus Christ and, with God's help, intend to continue living that faith in the Catholic church. I promise to do all in my power to share the faith I have received with our children by having them baptized and reared as Catholics." Kevin did sign the document, but he changed "to do all in my power" to "to the best of my ability."

In any case, interfaith marriages are allowed and may even be performed jointly in another church with the participation of a priest and another clergyman. Although the Catholic wedding ceremony is usually held in a church, it is possible to obtain permission to have the service celebrated in a home or garden. Weddings are usually not planned on Sundays or during Lent, although special permissions are sometimes granted.

The controversial question of divorce and remarriage has not changed along with these other reforms. Quite simply, unless a Catholic is widowed or has been granted an annulment by the church, she or he may not remarry with the blessings of the church.

The Jewish Ceremony

The Jewish wedding, from ancient times to the present, encompasses three main elements: (1) *ketubah* ("wedding contract"); (2) a gift of value, usually a ring, given by the groom to his bride; and (3) consummation or cohabitation, as symbolized by the *huppah* ("canopy") which represents the couple's home. These and other wedding traditions may be interpreted differently by Orthodox, Conservative, or Reform Jews. The Orthodox approach is strict and traditional, the Conservative less rigid, and the Reform quite liberal. As in other religions, Jewish couples are once again opting for the more traditional ritual rather than some neutralized version of the ceremony, but even a classic Jewish wedding offers choices.

Before the ceremony, the groom may celebrate with his friends by taking food and drink from a special table, called a *chassan's tisch.* This tradition is akin to a stag party and is not a mandatory feature of the wedding, but the signing of the *ketubah,* or marriage contract, is essential.

Originally, the *ketubah* was a simple monetary agreement between the groom and the bride's father. The bride was considered a form of property, and the document formalized the transaction. But when the ancient rabbis realized that divorce left women bereft and impoverished, the contract was changed to provide for the wife's well-being. Since there were no laws to protect women and children from abandonment, the *ketubah* did then what a court of law does now—insured the fair distribution of property and wealth in the event of separation.

Written in Aramaic as well as in English, the following traditional *ketubah* is still used today in Orthodox marriages:

> This is to Certify
>
> That on the ______ day of the week, the ______ day of the month ______ in the year ______ corresponding to the ______ day of 19____, the holy Covenant of Marriage was entered into, in ______ between the Bridegroom ______ and his Bride ______.
>
> The said bridegroom made the following declaration to his bride: "Be thou my wife according to the laws of Moses and of Israel. I faithfully promise that I will be a true husband unto thee. I will honor and cherish thee. I will work for thee. I will protect and support thee, and will provide all that is necessary for thy due sustenance, even as it becomes a Jewish husband to do. I also take upon myself all such further obligations for thy maintenance as are prescribed by our religious statute."
>
> And the bride has plighted her troth unto him, in affection and sincerity, and has thus taken upon herself the fulfillment of all the duties incumbent upon a Jewish wife.
>
> This Covenant of Marriage was duly executed and witnessed this day according to the usage of Israel.
>
> Rabbi ______ Witnesses ______
>
> ______

As you may expect, some people think this document has little to do with today's dual-income couple whose instincts are to share alike.

Here's how one couple created their own *ketubah*. The bride is the daughter of a prominent American rabbi. The groom is an Israeli.

> On Sunday, the 3rd of Elul, in the year 1979, in the community of family and friends gathered here in Sands Point in the state of New York, in the U.S.A.
>
> The bridegroom, Elan, son of Eitan and Edith Ezrachi, said to the bride, Naamah, daughter of Wolfe and Jacky Kelman: "Be my wife according to the laws of Moses and Israel. Take this ring as a

token of my hand in yours, always. As we unfold the story of our lives, we come together like our families today, to be part of one people's history, Israel's, as alive today as always, and to share our future like chapters woven into one book. I give myself to you like an open book, to share the good parts with the bad, my successes and my failures.

"Let the home we are building be as filled with Israel's light as with the Jewish trust in people, and let it rise on the foundations of devotion to Zion and love of people.

"I will open my heart to you always: lit by my love, radiant with my faith, illuminated by my soul."

And the bride responded:

"Be my husband according to the laws of Moses and Israel. With this ring I am part of you as I am part of Israel—together we are whole in a Jewish family. Let our lives keep close as body and soul, our hearts stay together like breath and spirit.

"Let us turn together to face our disappointments, embrace our dreams, realize our hopes, and accept our failures.

"Let the pillars of our home be: Torah, Mitzvot, and Loving-kindness. Let the air we breathe be as sustaining as the spirit and tradition of Israel. And let the warmth we radiate be a reflection of the radiance within the people of Israel.

"I will open my heart to you always: lit by my love, radiant with my faith, illuminated by my soul."

The bride and bridegroom promise one another to aspire to these ideals throughout their lives together, through mutual understanding, openness, and sensitivity to each other; to be conscious of what they share and what they don't, to what brings them together and what separates.

Therefore the couple is committed to provide for one another and to support one another in their combined and separate creativity.

Elan and Naamah wrote a contract not unlike Kevin and Debra's Prayer of the Couple for their Catholic wedding. According to one prominent rabbi, because the *ketubah* is a contract, it is always negotiable between the two parties, as long as it violates no Jewish laws.

After the invocation, the *erusin* ("betrothal blessing") is said. Here, under the bridal canopy and in the presence of ten male witnesses (a *minyan*), the wine and ring are blessed, and the couple drinks from the first cup of wine. Then, the ring (or rings) is exchanged. Some Orthodox rabbis will not permit the double ring ceremony because only the groom is supposed to offer something of value that he legally owns.

At this point the *ketubah* may be read aloud, followed by the recital of the seven benedictions over the second cup of wine. The rabbi, the cantor, or other members of the community may read these blessings. The couple then sips from the second goblet of wine.

The couple is now married, but before the joy and feasting begin, a glass is shattered to symbolize the destruction of the Temple that took place at least two thousand years ago. According to a story in the Talmud, a sage had prepared a wedding feast for his son: "He observed that the rabbis present were very gay. So he seized a costly goblet worth four hundred zuzim and broke it before them. Thus he made them sober."

The Jewish ceremony can take place almost anywhere. Many are held in synagogues, but the service can be performed at home, in a garden, or at a club, hall, or hotel. Marriages are not held on Saturday, the Sabbath.

No Orthodox or Conservative rabbi will permit an interfaith marriage unless the non-Jew converts, but some Reform rabbis do not require conversion. Two male witnesses—often the rabbi and the cantor—are the minimum required at all Jewish wedding ceremonies.

Other questions, such as whether the service is recited in Hebrew (traditional) or English, must be discussed with your rabbi. The rabbi may also wish to offer a homily about marriage and the couple. This idea personalizes the service and is acceptable to most clergymen.

The Protestant Ceremony

Because there are so many sects within Protestantism, it is difficult to list any absolute rules or options concerning the wedding ceremony. The traditional service is taken from *The Book of Common Prayer,* which was updated in 1979. In that version, the word *obey* was replaced by *comfort.*

Although the Episcopal church does not allow any change in the marriage vows, they may be lenient about music, prayer offerings, readings, and "giving away" of the bride. Most Protestant ceremonies start with a prayerful explanation of the purpose of the ceremony. "Dearly beloved, we are gathered together in the sight of God" is the traditional introduction. Then, the minister charges the couple to declare their intentions of lifelong marriage. ("Wilt thou have this woman as thy wedded wife?") The marriage vows are then recited, followed by the exchange of rings. The minister offers prayers (including the Lord's Prayer, if desired), declares the couple married, and concludes with a benediction.

Following are the traditional vows from *The Book of Common Prayer* and an alternative suggested to one couple by their Lutheran Church.

> I, _____, take thee, _____ to be my wedded wife/husband, to have and to hold from this day forward, for better for worse, for richer for poorer, in sickness and in health, to love and to cherish, till death us do part, according to God's holy ordinance; thereto I plight thee my troth.

> _____, I take you to be my wife/husband from this time onward, to join with you and to share all that is to come, to give and to receive, to speak and to listen, to inspire and to respond, and in all circumstances of our life together to be loyal to you with my whole life and with my whole being.

In the Protestant faith, interfaith marriages are usually no problem, although one partner must be a baptized Protestant of that sect. Divorced people can remarry, but they must show proof of a legal divorce. Some Episcopal churches insist on a "church judgment" as well as a state divorce. Many Protestant sects now have female clerics who can perform the marriage ceremony. If this is your choice, check with your local parish to see if you can arrange for a female officiant.

Eastern Orthodox Ceremonies

Greek, Russian, Lebanese, and Romanian people, as well as other Mediterranean and Eastern groups, are part of the constituency that makes up the membership of the Eastern Orthodox Church. The heritage and tradition are close to the Roman Catholic and Episcopal faiths, but patriarchs, rather than a pope, form the leadership of the church.

Depending on the priest and the type of community, the Orthodox wedding service may be conducted in English, another language, or both. The priest has the discretion to permit any changes in or additions to the ceremony, but because the service is lengthy and steeped in Byzantine ritual, editing is not encouraged.

The altar is separated from the body of the church by the iconostasis (a screen of painted icons), and the ceremony takes place in front of the Holy Doors leading to the altar and sanctuary. Here, a table is placed, on which rests a Bible, a wine chalice, a cross, candles, and flowers. Throughout the ceremony, the bride and groom hold candles that symbolize the Lord's light, and the bride's bouquet is either placed on the table or held by an attendant. Also, wreaths or crowns are placed on the couple's heads, and they walk around the table three times to honor the Trinity. If the bride is wearing a headpiece that won't accommodate the crown, it must be removed and held by an attendant.

Interfaith marriages are permitted, but one partner and one witness must be Eastern Orthodox. The church also requires that Orthodox members receive Holy Communion on the Sunday preceding the marriage. Divorced people can remarry in the church, but an ecclesiastical decree is required.

Nondenominational Ceremonies

Couples who want the spiritual essence of a marriage ceremony without the structure of a formal religion can turn to a nondenominational organization such as the Unitarian church or the Society for Ethical Culture. Here, a philosophy—rather than a creed or series of laws—creates a spiritual environment in which people may pray without ritual and have faith without doctrine. Christians, Jews, and others make up the congregation.

The marriage service offered by the Community Church of New York (Unitarian) begins with a reading from the Book of Ruth and a passage from Kahlil Gibran's *The Prophet.* Then, in a simple yet traditional way, the ceremony continues as follows:

> "We are gathered together to unite this man and this woman in marriage, which is an institution founded in nature, ordained by

the state, sanctioned by the church or synagogue, and made honorable by the faithful keeping of good men and women in all ages. It is, therefore, not by any to be entered into unadvisedly or lightly, but discreetly, advisedly, and with due reverence. This celebration is an outward token of a sacred and inward union of hearts, which the church or synagogue may bless and the state make legal, but which neither can create or annul, a union created by your loving purpose and kept by your abiding will. Into this estate these two persons come to be united.

"Is it in this spirit and for this purpose that you have come hither to be joined together?"

"It is."

"Do you ______, take ______, to be your wife/husband, to love and to cherish, to honor and to comfort, in sickness or in health, in sorrow or in joy, in hardship or in ease, to have and to hold from this day forth?"

"I do."

Then, after the blessing of the ring or rings, the couple say the following: "With this ring I thee wed, and pledge thee my faithful love. Amen." A prayer is offered before the couple are declared husband and wife, and the benediction follows.

Nondenominational ceremonies can take place anywhere, at any time, and there is no problem for divorced people who are remarrying. A couple can suggest their own poems or prayer readings, and the vows can be amended or edited in any reasonable way.

The Civil Ceremony

The civil ceremony is an adaptation from *The Book of Common Prayer* and has been modernized at most City Halls. It takes approximately sixty-six seconds, and it seems, at the very least, an ascetic ritual. But some couples want only the straight and narrow legal wedding. As one bride explained, "I believe you marry in small ways over a long period of time. The ceremony is part of the marriage process."

Still, if you marry anywhere outside of City Hall, the judge or justice will usually allow you to create a more elaborate ceremony and may even collaborate with you by offering his or her own articulation on the subject of marriage.

If you find a willing civil officiant, you can be married anywhere, at any time, as long as you come prepared with the documents required by the state.

Processionals and Recessionals

The processional at a traditional Christian wedding starts with the ushers; then come the bridesmaids, the maid and matron of honor, the flower girl and ringbearer, and the bride, who is escorted by her father. This arrangement can be changed in any way you prefer. You can walk down the aisle with your fiancé instead of having him and the best man wait for you at the altar. You can walk with both your parents; he can walk with his, etc. One Catholic priest told of calling the names of the bride and groom, who were seated with the congregation. They advanced to the altar and the ceremony began. The recessional starts with the bride and groom, followed by pairs of ushers and bridesmaids, or a simple repeat of the processional arrangement.

At Jewish weddings, the rabbi and cantor lead the way (or they may await the processional at the *huppah*), followed by the bride's grandparents, the groom's grandparents, the ushers, the best man, the groom flanked by his parents, the bridesmaids, the maid or matron of honor, and finally, the bride flanked by her parents. There are many variations of this arrangement, and they must be discussed with your rabbi. The traditional Jewish recessional begins with the couple, followed by the bride's parents, the groom's parents, the rabbi and cantor, the grandparents, the honor attendants, the matron of honor, any children, bridesmaids, and ushers.

If you're having a religious wedding that some of the guests might not understand, you may want to provide a simple photocopied program of the prayers, hymns, and vows as they will occur during the ceremony. Some people think this adds understanding and impact by allowing people to read the traditions and rituals. But the printed program can distract people, too, drawing their eyes away from the altar or *huppah* and into the fine print. Think carefully before plunging ahead.

Remember that the role of the wedding guest is to bear witness to your wedding—not to participate in it. Close friends, especially attendants, and family members may be asked to read Scripture or verse, but don't expect the guests to hold hands and chant for world peace without feeling put-upon or embarrassed.

8 · The Invitations

Preparing the Guest List

In some communities it is common to have a big church wedding followed by a reception in the church hall. The reception consists of a receiving line, a large wedding cake, and coffee or punch. Guests come in, shake hands with the family, have a piece of cake and a drink, and leave after 15 or 20 minutes. This is not the most gracious wedding reception. People dress up, make an effort to get to the church, and send a wedding gift, and at the least, they ought to be offered a choice of drinks, hors d'oeuvres, or a meal.

The one thing this type of wedding accomplishes is not having to limit the guest list because of money. But for those couples who want to offer their guests more substantial fare, the budget will determine how many people to invite, thus dictating the style of your wedding. If five hundred of your nearest and dearest are to be assembled, for example, you'll want to have a superformal wedding with all the pageantry and tradition you can muster—engraved invitations, a lavish reception, lots of bridesmaids and ushers, and a dramatic wedding dress. But if fifty people is your choice or your financial limit, tailor the wedding to that number.

Traditionally, the guest list is split between the two families, with the bride's parents, as hosts, setting the limit. If the wedding is being financed by both families, they decide jointly how many guests to invite, and they split the list accordingly. Obviously, when the bride and groom are paying, it is they who control the numbers.

In today's economy, few can afford not to limit the number of guests, but figuring out who comes and who doesn't can make you feel like a ruthless Machiavellian who commits social genocide by concentrating solely on the "A" list. Should all second cousins be categorically eliminated? If you ask one friend from the office, will they all expect an invitation? Are hurt feelings inevitable?

When I was planning my first wedding, all these questions began to plague me, and I really thought that my family and a lot of friends would never forgive us for what we were about to do. My mother was a widow with limited resources, and my fiancé and I had little to contribute. We estimated that we could only include our immediate families and close friends, totaling about forty-five people. The idea was to have the wedding at my hometown church and the reception at the rather large penthouse apartment I shared with roommates in town.

Here's how we handled the situation. My mother called all the relatives and hometown friends who would have been invited under other circumstances, told them about the marriage, explained that the reception would be limited to the immediate families and closest of friends, and invited them to come to the church for the ceremony. Bob and I made similar calls to friends. On my wedding day, as I approached the center aisle on my brother's arm, the church was packed. It looked like Easter Sunday rather than a Saturday in June. And even though a chosen few were invited to the reception, a sense of goodwill and celebration prevailed.

No matter what the etiquette books say, inviting people to the ceremony and not the reception should never be done with formal, engraved invitations. It's a sure way of creating bad feelings. People might be hurt if they feel that you spent money on fancy invitations, but not on them. A telephone invitation, on the other hand, is a casual, personal way of saying we'd like to see you at church—and no gift is expected.

Conversely, some couples prefer a private ceremony followed by a large reception. In this case, the invitations can be as formal or casual as the party suggests.

Begin by making a list of everyone you know, and dividing it into three parts: family, friends, and business or professional associates. Go through your address book and calendar, noting all the cocktail, dinner, and weekend invitations you've accepted during the last year, and include the names of those hosts. Consult with your parents for a list of family members. Indicate with an asterisk those who live out of town. You can assume that about half the out-of-towners will decline the invitation, and you can reapportion the numbers accordingly.

Now the hard part begins—coding the list into three groups: A, B, and C. The A's are musts for invitations; the B's are probables; the C's are optional. Your fiancé and his family should do the same, and when the names are in, you'll have a realistic idea of the numbers. If the A list totals 100 people and that fabulous restaurant only holds 75 comfortably, find another place for the reception. Or if A and B combined are under the budgetary limit, throw it open to the C's.

The A group consists of people you absolutely love, people who were there when you needed them, people who are important links in the family network, anyone who will be hosting or attending a party in your honor, the clergyman or judge—anyone who, if they weren't invited, would be truly missed by you. There are some people who merit an A rating simply because of their family standing—such as old Uncle Charlie. Maybe he doesn't have much to do with your life, but he represents a link between the generations, reinforcing the notion of tradition and ritual. If you hate Uncle Charlie, you don't have to invite him, but a neutral feeling or better should get him to the wedding.

Sticky Situations

Kids. Either for reasons of budget or peace of mind, you may not want children at your wedding who are, say, under 8 years old. Most people won't assume that their kids are invited unless their children's names appear on the invitations, but it doesn't hurt to spread the word that costs and space will limit the kid list. Your only rule is to not make exceptions in favor of a special niece or nephew. Your own children, or younger brothers and sisters, however, should definitely be at your wedding.

If you can accommodate children, it's rewarding to have all the generations represented at your wedding. And if a little one decides to gurgle or cry when you say "I do," it will make the whole experience more human. Said one bride, "The best moment of the day was seeing all the children gathered round the wedding cake looking longingly at the rich white icing and creamy pink rosebuds. Norman Rockwell couldn't have painted a more perfect picture, and I have the photograph to prove it."

Special interest groups. Should you invite everyone on the bowling team, and would they and their spouses want to come? You can invite one, not all, and you shouldn't be embarrassed into inviting people you don't like. Bowling teams, fellow students in adult education classes, PBS fund-raising cronies, and your old teachers at Lincoln High do not a wedding make.

The premature gift. You might receive a gift from an acquaintance who is not on the list. Even though wedding invitations usually result in wedding gifts, the reverse is not necessarily true. Giving a gift doesn't mean you're automatically invited to the wedding. What to do? Send a thank-you note with a suggestion of getting together after the wedding. The truth about weddings is that no one should presume an invitation, and you shouldn't try to pay off social debts or gain professional stature by guilefully sending out invitations. One friend of mine, an editor of a national magazine, was baffled to receive an invitation to the wedding of a writer he had met only once at a cocktail party. He concluded, and was probably right, that the writer was looking for a professional "in."

Two disparate families—separate but equal. One bride struggled with the notion of merging her own upper-middle-class suburban family with her fiancé's ethnic urban clan. First of all, both families were enormous, and the wedding, she felt, would become a three-ring circus.

In addition, she didn't think his family would feel comfortable or relaxed in her family's country club milieu. Her solution was to have one big country club prewedding party, one big bash at his family's favorite neighborhood restaurant, and one real wedding where the immediate families and close friends had the time of their lives.

Reciprocal invitations. So-and-so invited you to their wedding and would be terribly hurt, etc. Here the numbers count. It's nice to invite anyone who had you to their wedding, but if you're sticking with family and close friends only, you don't have to reciprocate.

Inviting people to your wedding is not like planning a fabulous dinner party where guests are carefully selected for their scintillating conversation or appealing wit. This is one event where history and tradition override your social instincts to bring together the best and brightest. And don't fret about disparate social groups. The common bond of affection toward you and your fiancé is all that's needed for people to get along and have a good time.

Odd couples. They're living together and you can't stand him: consider them engaged and invite him.

Homosexual couples. If one person is your friend and you haven't met his or her housemate, you're not obliged to send two invitations. If, however, you know them as a couple, both get invited.

Wording the Invitations

How to invite people to your wedding has become a matter of raging debate during the past few years. Confusion reigns. Traditionalists and conservatives want engraved invitations, black on white or cream. They dismiss enclosed reply cards as tacky and insulting, and any change in traditional wording is as heinous a crime as rewriting the Bill of Rights. At the other extreme is the crafty couple whose last course in silk-screening inspires them to issue invitations on recycled paper or fake scrolls with such words as, "Ophelia and Romeo want to spend their lives together. Please come and celebrate their joy with us." etc. Invitations like these make you suspect that you will be asked to join hands in a circle of love and peace while the couple recites interminable passages from Kahlil Gibran.

As one groom said, "The seriousness with which the couple takes their wedding is reflected in the whole attitude of the guests. People are not going to come to your wedding in a jogging suit if they receive a formal, engraved invitation."

It is true that your invitations are the first step in setting the style of your wedding. And happily, between the extremes lies a cornucopia of possibilities. The following chart outlines the most commonly used invitation options.

Printing Techniques and Processes

Engraving. Used for formal invitations, engraving is the most expensive way to go. Invitations alone (without enclosure cards) cost anywhere from $1.00 to $2.50 each. The results, however, are impressive. Raised letters, created from hand-engraved plates, appear on thick, creamy paper. Tissues protect the engraved lines, which can be ordered in colors at an extra charge.

Thermography. It's printing, but the letters are embossed so that it looks engraved. Colored paper and lettering are available, and the wording can be formal or innovative. Cost: about $50 per hundred.

Offset Printing. Can be used for nontraditional weddings on any kind of paper, cards, postcards, or posters. Cost: about $50 per hundred, depending on paper, color, etc.

Photocopying. Superinformal and very cheap. Colored Xerox copiers are available at a higher rate per sheet. Photocopying is best used for maps, transportation schedules, or other diagrams included in formal invitations. Cost: (b/w) $5.00 per hundred; (color) $45 per hundred.

Handwritten. For twenty-five to fifty guests, this is the best choice. Paper and wording can be formal or not, but the handwriting, with a fine-tip felt or fountain pen, should be impeccable.

Novelties. Printed balloons, T-shirts, singing telegrams, picture postcards, cartoon strips—all are possible for casual weddings. But here are words to the wise: if they're cute rather than clever, people will be turned off.

Formal Traditional Invitations

Formal invitations are issued by the people hosting the wedding and reception and are sent four to six weeks before the wedding. Traditionally, the bride's parents are the hosts, but in instances of divorced parents, shared expenses, and couples paying for their own weddings, the wording logically changes.

A combination ceremony and reception invitation might read as follows:

Mr. and Mrs. John Doe
request the honour of your presence
at the marriage of their daughter
Patricia
to
Mr. Robert Aldrich Peters
on Saturday, the first of May
One thousand nine hundred and eighty-two
at twelve o'clock
St. Mary's Church
and at the reception
following the ceremony
The Peach Club
Atlanta, Georgia

R.S.V.P.

I don't think people should receive formal invitations to a church ceremony only, but if you disagree, the invitation would include a reception card and could read as follows:

Mr. and Mrs. John Doe
request the honour of your presence
at the marriage of their daughter
Patricia
to
Mr. Robert Aldrich Peters
on Saturday, the first of May
One thousand nine hundred and eighty-two
at twelve o'clock
St. Mary's Church
Atlanta

And the reception card would read:

Reception
Immediately following the Ceremony
The Peach Club
Atlanta, Georgia

The Favour of a Reply is Requested
(address optional)

The honour (British spelling) *of your presence* implies a religious ceremony.

The pleasure of your company is used for civil weddings that are held in gardens, at home, in clubs, etc., and it is also used on reception invitations.

With the exception of Mr. and Mrs. (Ms., if you like), almost everything is written out. Jr. or junior, Dr. or Doctor is acceptable, and Mr. and Mrs. John Smith, 3rd, is okay. The time (half after four o'clock); short street addresses (Fifteen Elm Street); names (Thomas Stearns Eliot, not T. S. Eliot); and dates (the eighth of September).

Don't edit the name of your church. If the logo is St. Peter's don't write Saint.

If your parents are divorced, and they're both hosting your wedding, the invitation should read *Mrs. Anderson Doe,* for it is traditional to include your mother's maiden name; *Mrs. Jane Doe;* or, if she has assumed her maiden name, *Ms. Jane Anderson and Mr. John Doe. . . .*

If your mother or father is remarried, invitations can be sent in your mother's name only, by her and her husband, or by both couples, depending on how everyone feels about the stepparents.

With both parents hosting the wedding, note that the RSVP should include the name and address of the parent who will be tabulating the replies. It would read: *R.S.V.P. Mrs. Smith, Fifteen Elm Street.*

If a divorced parent is the only host, it reads *the honour of your presence is requested at the marriage of her (his) daughter,* etc. (Or, *Mrs. Smith's daughter* is sometimes used if Mr. and Mrs. Smith issue the invitation. In this case, the bride's full name is included in the invitation.)

If your mother is a widow, her name is *Mrs. John Doe* on the invitation.

If brothers, sisters, grandparents, aunts, or uncles sponsor your wedding, they can indicate *the marriage of their sister, their niece,* or *her granddaughter.* A more remote relationship is not indicated on the invitation, and in most cases the bride's full name will appear, since, with the exception of a brother, the names of most relatives will be different.

You can imagine the variations of formal invitations as divorces, living arrangements, or other social changes start to branch out on the family tree. If your married sister and single brother want to host your wedding, for example, the invitation might read: *Mrs. Alice Doe Fitch and Mr. Thomas Doe request the honour of your presence at the marriage of their sister. . . .*

If your parents and his are cosponsoring the wedding, the invitation could read: *Mr. and Mrs. John Doe and Mr. and Mrs. Charles Peters request the honour of your presence at the marriage of Patricia Doe and Robert Aldrich Peters. . . .* Some people prefer to say *their children, Patricia and Robert,* but it's better to be an adult when you're getting married.

Some new etiquette guides suggest that if the bride and groom are helping to finance their own wedding, they should send invitations that say: *We join our parents, Jane and John Doe and Martha and Charles Peters, in inviting you to share our happiness as we exchange marriage vows. . . .* An invitation like this is confusing to those who don't know the parents. Why not give your parents a break and let them have the floor on this one. Otherwise, go the whole route and issue the invitations yourselves.

If you are the hosts, you have the following choices:

The honour of your presence
is requested at the marriage of
Miss Patricia Doe
to

Mr. Robert Aldrich Peters
on Saturday, the first of May
at twelve o'clock
St. Mary's Church
and afterward at
The Peach Club
Atlanta, Georgia

R.S.V.P.
Miss Doe
One Main Street

. . .

Ms. Patricia Doe
and
Mr. Robert Aldrich Peters
request the honour of your presence
at their marriage
on Saturday, the first of May
at twelve o'clock
St. Mary's Church
and afterward at
The Peach Club
Atlanta, Georgia

. . .

Ms. Patricia Doe
and
Mr. Robert Aldrich Peters
invite you to their wedding
on Saturday, the first of May
at twelve o'clock
St. Mary's Church
and afterward at
The Peach Club
Atlanta, Georgia

One bride who paid for her own wedding wanted the invitations issued in her parents' names. The ceremony and reception took place at the house of a friend in New York, and her parents lived in San Antonio, Texas. Here's how she handled it:

Mr. and Mrs. Henry Joseph Denk
request the honour of your presence
at the marriage of their daughter
Patricia Ruth
to
Mr. William Michael Powers
Saturday, the eighteenth of August
One thousand nine hundred and seventy-nine
at five o'clock
at the home of Mr. and Mrs. Wilfrid Sheed
Sag Harbor, Long Island, New York

What worried Patricia most was that people would respond to her in New York rather than to her mother in San Antonio. Her solution was to enclose a separate card that read:

The favour of a reply is requested
102 Pepper Bush Lane
San Antonio, Texas 78231

Even though I don't approve of sending engraved invitations to the ceremony only (and separate reception cards to a select few), I think it's fine to reverse the process for those couples who want a very private ceremony and a large reception. Here's how to proceed. The large folded invitation would read as follows:

The pleasure of your company
is requested at the wedding reception of
Miss Patricia Doe
and
Mr. Robert Aldrich Peters
on Saturday, the first of May
at one o'clock
The Peach Club
Atlanta, Georgia

R.S.V.P.
Miss Doe
One Main Street

And tucked inside, the ceremony card would read:

The honour of your presence
is requested at the marriage ceremony
at twelve o'clock
Atlanta

Second weddings for divorced or widowed brides used to be restricted to whispered phone invitations or discreet handwritten notes. It is true that most people marrying again sponsor their own weddings, but any of the forms shown above are perfectly acceptable.

Military titles follow standard protocol rules for both men and women. Enlisted people and noncommissioned officers can note their branch of service underneath their name, but it's optional: *Robert Aldrich Peters, United States Army.* For high-ranking officers (captain or above in the army; lieutenant, senior grade, or above in the navy), titles precede the name, and the branch of service is written on the line beneath. Lower-ranking officers list the name on the top line, their title and branch beneath.

Double wedding invitations often involve two sisters. Such an invitation could read as follows: *Mr. and Mrs. John Doe request the honour of your presence at the marriage of their daughters, Patricia to Mr. Robert Aldrich Peters, and Mary Sue to Mr. Thomas Anderson. . . .* If the brides in a double wedding are simply friends, both sets of parents' names appear. Traditionally, the older bride's name appears first (therefore her parents' names would top the invitation). You may instead choose alphabetical order, or simply toss a coin.

Enclosures

Pew cards are superformal and work like theater tickets with seat assignments. The first come, first served approach is usually less complicated. But if your wedding is large, a simple handwritten "Pew no. F" could be enclosed.

Admission cards are not necessary unless the ceremony is being held at a public place, such as a museum or church that has become a national landmark. Such cards might read: *Please present this card at the Smithsonian Institution, Saturday, the first of June.*

At-home cards are usually sent with announcements and, since many couples have been living together before their marriages and don't need to announce their new address, are fast going out of style. They read as follows: *At home after May fifteenth, 315 East 72nd Street, New York City.* Or: *Mr. and Mrs. Robert Peters will be at home. . . .* Or, if the bride is not changing her name: *Jane Doe and Robert Peters will be at home. . . .*

Reply cards are considered déclassé and dehumanizing, and some people are insulted when they receive them in any formal invitation. Truth is, though, they're terribly convenient, and they hasten replies that otherwise would dribble in slowly. If you decide to use them, make sure you also include hand-addressed, stamped envelopes. One bride who decided to use the cards was surprised when most of them were returned with such personal comments as, "Of course we'll be there," or "Wouldn't miss it." She concluded that the austere accept______ regret______ was too businesslike for the occasion, so she designed a new form:

(Guest's name handwritten here)
For your convenience, we're enclosing this card.
_____ accept
_____ regret
Thank you for your prompt reply.

Maps or directions can be photocopied and enclosed with invitations or sent separately to those who have accepted the invitation.

Name Cards. If you're not changing your name at all or intend to join names through hyphenation, you can enclose a card that says the following:

Patricia Doe
will retain her surname
after her marriage to
Robert A. Peters
Your cooperation in this regard
is appreciated

If you and he wish to combine names, you can say: *Patricia and Robert, after marriage, will share the surname Doe-Peters.*

How to Respond to Formal Invitations

If people don't know your parents, they could follow the formal reply, which parrots the invitation and is usually written on formal notepaper.

Mr. and Mrs. Warren Smith
accept with pleasure
Mr. and Mrs. John Doe's
kind invitation for
Saturday, the first of May
at twelve o'clock.

Or: . . . *regret that they are unable to accept the kind invitation of Mr. and Mrs. John Doe.* They may also send a more personal note: *Dear Jane and John, Warren and I are happy to accept your kind invitation to Patricia and Robert's wedding.*

New Wave Invitations

Contemporary invitations have a warmer approach, but they can be sappy and sentimental, too. Beware of such phrases as *want to go through life together; Jim and Judy are in love; ultimate experience; festival of life;* or *the union of man and woman.*

In their own way, these all-embracing phrases can be as disconcerting as the rigid traditional forms. It's okay to share joy or happiness, but no one should be expected to "share the experience" of your wedding. Most people are there as observers and witnesses to your personal rite of passage. Don't make the invitation sound like a California therapy that gets you in touch with your feelings about heterosexual coupling.

Instead, consider simplifying the language and style to conform to modern usage. If you like, sans serif typefaces and block paragraphs can be used in lieu of centered lines and formal lettering.

The examples below are written as block paragraphs, but it's also fine to use the traditional format with modern wording. If your parents are hosting the wedding, the invitations might read in the following ways:

(1) John and Jane Doe invite you to celebrate the wedding of their daughter Patricia to John Peters on Saturday. . . .

(2) Please join us in celebrating our daughter Patricia's marriage to John Peters on Saturday, May first, at twelve o'clock, at St. Mary's Church. A reception will follow at the Peach Club. (signed) John and Jane Doe.

(3) John and Jane Doe invite you to share in the joy of the marriage of

their daughter Patricia to Robert Aldrich Peters, Saturday, the first of May. . . .

(4) We'd be honored to have you attend the wedding of our daughter Patricia to Robert Aldrich Peters, Saturday, May first. . . . (signed) John and Jane Doe.

(5) Our daughter Patricia will marry John Peters on Saturday, May first, at St. Mary's Church, at twelve o'clock. Please join us at the ceremony and reception afterward at the Peach Club. (signed) John and Mary Doe.

(6) We're happy to invite you to the marriage of our daughter Patricia and John Peters on Saturday, May first, at twelve o'clock, at St. Mary's Church, and at the reception afterward at the Peach Club. (signed) John and Mary Doe.

If you are sending out your own invitations, you may edit any of the forms above or create your own message. Here's one idea:

Patricia Doe and Robert Peters
invite you to share in the celebration
of their wedding
Saturday, the first of May
at twelve o'clock
St. Mary's Church
and at the reception
following the ceremony
The Peach Club
Atlanta, Georgia

R.S.V.P.

Don't hesitate to choose colored or tinted papers and type for your personalized invitations. Chances are, though, that some engravers will not accommodate the less traditional styles. If not, a reliable printer is your best choice.

Handwritten Invitations for Small Weddings

Handwritten invitations read like personal notes and are sent by the host(s).

Dear Michael and Barbara,

Patricia will marry Robert Peters on Saturday, May first, at St. Mary's Church. The ceremony will take place at noon, and the reception will follow here at home. Please join us for this happy occasion.

As ever,
Jane

. . .

Dear Michael and Barbara,

Patricia and Robert will be married at home on Saturday, May first, at noon. Please join us at the ceremony and reception to follow.

Love,
Jane

. . .

Dear Michael and Barbara,

Robert and I will be married at our apartment on Saturday, May first, at noon. We'd be so happy if you could join us for the ceremony and reception to follow.

Love,
Patricia

Telephone invitations are appropriate for small weddings, too. Just make sure everyone has the necessary information and calls back with a response if they can't commit on the spot.

Wedding Announcements

Wedding announcements are usually sent to people who are not invited to the ceremony and reception. They simply inform people of the marriage and carry no obligation for gifts. They're especially useful when the wedding is small. They should be mailed as near to the date of the wedding as possible, and that means addressing envelopes in advance. Announcements follow any of the forms of invitation, both formal and contemporary, and may include at-home cards. Don't forget to include the year the wedding took place.

Mr. and Mrs. John Doe
have the honour of
announcing the marriage of their daughter
Patricia
to
Mr. Robert Aldrich Peters
Saturday, the first of May
One thousand nine hundred and eighty-two
Atlanta, Georgia

You can announce your own marriage, as can both sets of parents, friends, or any other person who has sponsored the wedding. If the formal style doesn't appeal to you, personalize the wording.

We are happy to announce
our marriage
on Saturday, the first of May
1982
Atlanta, Georgia

Patricia Doe and Robert Peters

Addressing and Mailing

The formal wedding invitation has two envelopes. The outer envelope (which is sealed for mailing) has a handwritten or embossed return address on the flap. The unsealed inner envelope contains the invitation (engraved side up) and any enclosure cards. Remove the protective tissue before mailing. If you're including reply cards, a stamped, addressed envelope with reply card inserted is enclosed separately from the invitation.

Since penmanship counts when addressing envelopes, choose a fine felt tip or fountain pen to match the color of the printing and engraving, and select a pretty commemorative stamp. The outer envelope is addressed with a minimum of abbreviation. (Follow the same standards as on the invitations, but don't spell out the zip code!) The inner envelope repeats the last name(s) only.

The following chart gives the latest etiquette on how to address married people, singles, cohabitants, children, and homosexual couples. The column on the left illustrates how to address the outer envelopes; the one on the right, the inside envelopes.

Married couples who share a name

Mr. and Mrs. John Smith 104 Bayview Drive Asbury Park, New Jersey 87041	Mr. and Mrs. Smith

Married couples with two different names

Ms. Angela Banks Mr. John Smith (*alphabetically listed*) 104 Bayview Drive Asbury Park, New Jersey 87041	Ms. Banks and Mr. Smith

Single People

Mr. Charles Helms	Mr. Helms
Ms. (Mrs.) Carol Clark (divorcée)	Ms. Clark
Mrs. Stanley Clark (widow)	Mrs. Clark

Children

If they're sixteen or over (some prefer eighteen), children receive their own invitations. Under that age, you may send them their own or handle it as follows:

Mr. and Mrs. John Smith 104 Bayview Drive Asbury Park, New Jersey 87041	Mr. and Mrs. Smith Sean and Marcv

Never write "and family," which is confusing and may result in a party of ten.

Unmarried couples

Mr. Edward Lang Ms. Alice Washington (*alphabetically listed*) 210 East 15th Street New York, New York 10067	Mr. Lang and Ms. Washington

Homosexual couples

Separate invitations can be sent, or, if you know them as a couple, one invitation is fine, alphabetically listed.

Mr. John Eagleton
Mr. Richard Sykes
57 Third Street
Washington, D.C. 20068

Mr. Eagleton and Mr. Sykes

9. The Cast

Just as in every other aspect of your wedding, the degree of formality and the number of guests invited will determine the size of your wedding party. If you want bridesmaids by the demidozen, be sure that they walk down a real church aisle in full view of about 150 or more guests. And the kind of pageantry that requires the services of a page boy, a ring bearer, a flower girl, a junior bridesmaid, and myriad ushers and bridesmaids suggests a very formal ceremony with 250 to 500 guests filling the pews.

Smaller first or second weddings are usually simplified in favor of a maid or matron of honor and a best man, although they can be attended by two men, two women, or any combination of children. When Ronald Reagan's son was married, an old friend and a secret service agent were the only witnesses. For my first wedding, held in a church with about one hundred people looking on, I had only a maid and matron of honor: my cousin and best friend, respectively. Three ushers and one best man attended the groom. For my second time around, a small wedding held in our own apartment, one good friend and two stepdaughters-to-be did the honors. And my husband's choice was jokingly referred to as the "second best man," since this was his second performance on my husband's behalf.

Unless you're spitefully neglecting a sibling or good friend, your friends won't be insulted if they are not asked to participate in your wedding. Often your very closest friend or favorite sister (or both) are asked to be honor attendants. Similarly, the groom's brother, friend, or even father can fill the role of best man. If you're adding bridesmaids and ushers to the cast, consider your future brothers- and sisters-in-law, as well as your own friends and relatives.

Most people think it an honor to participate in a wedding, and they'll usually go to some expense—both in time and money—to meet their responsibilities and to help make sure everything goes smoothly.

But it is my experience that without an organized script, members of the wedding tend to behave like passive spectators rather than active, responsible leaders. And since wedding rituals and styles vary so greatly today, you must prepare them to take charge of certain duties.

The Maid or Matron of Honor

In a traditional processional, your maid or matron of honor will precede you down the aisle. If necessary, she'll hold your bouquet and fix your veil and train. She is also on tap to help address invitations, make phone calls, do any reasonable preparation chores, and herd the other bridesmaids together for fittings. But her physical work contribution is rarely as important as her emotional support. As one bride recalled, "More than anything else she might have done, Sara put up with all my craziness, listened to my doubts and fears, and kept me going. My mother couldn't imagine why her 30-year-old daughter wasn't ecstatic about giving up her status as 'the only old maid left in the family.' And Mel was so confident about it all that I felt like a silly schoolgirl telling him everything on my mind. Sara was there when I really needed her."

The Bridesmaids

Bridesmaids have the cushiest time of it, being responsible for nothing more than the outfits they'll wear. All they have to do is show up on time for fittings, prewedding parties, rehearsals, and the wedding itself. But in some cases, especially at home or garden weddings, they'll act as secondary hostesses, introducing friends to family, making sure the champagne has been passed before any toasts are offered. Anyway, if you want them to do anything special, aside from posing for photographs, don't forget to tell them what you have in mind.

The Best Man

Ancient tradition suggests that the best man do everything for the groom except marry the bride and take her away. The assumption is that the groom is either too clumsy or too inept to remember how to dress, how to delegate responsibilities to the ushers, how to put the honeymoon luggage in the car, or how to wake up by himself on the morning of the wedding.

The best man is supposed to do a lot of hand holding while the groom does his share of hand wringing. Specifically, he's supposed to mobilize the ushers for the rehearsal and make sure they're at the wedding at least forty-five minutes in advance of the ceremony. He is in charge of the license, the ring, and slipping the check to the clergyman. He's allowed to join in the recessional by escorting the maid or matron of honor up the aisle, but then he has to forgo the receiving line at church in order to rush over to the reception and get the couples' luggage in the car! He's supposed to remind the groom to smile at Grandma Jones. He makes the first toast, reads the telegrams, and dances with the bride, the mothers, and the other female attendants.

Free at last? No way. He's also in charge of making sure the groom remembers to put his pants on while changing into his getaway clothes. Then comes his job as linebacker as the groom is leaving the reception under a shower of small objects such as rice or confetti.

If the groom is a hopeless drunk or a bumbling idiot, this kind of best man will get him through the wedding, but he can't do much for the marriage. If, on the other hand, the groom is over the age of 12 and sports an IQ in triple figures, he'll live up to his responsibilities without making his best friend a slave.

The Ushers

In order to expedite seating, you need at least one usher for every fifty people. As people enter the church, an usher will ask if they are friends of the bride or groom and then seat them accordingly. The bride's family and friends are seated to the left, the groom's to the right. The usher offers his arm to the woman, the man following behind. If there is a group, the usher escorts the oldest woman (if he can spot her), and the others follow. Toward the end of this seating period, if one or the other side of the church is out of balance, the ushers should even it up.

People who are assigned to reserved pews usually tell the ushers or present pew cards. Ushers memorize the numbers and seat people accordingly.

For traditionalists, the groom's mother is seated before the mother of the bride. Each gets an aisle seat. When the head usher escorts the bride's mother, it is a signal that the processional is about to begin. If the parents are cosponsors, the mothers can be escorted together by either the head usher or the groom's father (provided he is not in the wedding party).

Pairs of ushers are also responsible for laying the carpet and pew ribbons, generally helping people into cars after the ceremony, and posing for photographs. At home or garden weddings, the ushers can greet people, take coats (if necessary), and clear the ceremony area at the right time.

The Children

If there are flower girls, they will walk down the aisle just ahead of the bride. If a ring bearer is also in the wedding party, he carries the ring on a pillow, secured with thread. Unless the child is going to carry the actual ring, don't let him pose as a ringbearer. If you prefer that the best man be in charge of the ring, the little boy can still be in the wedding. Simply have him walk together with the flower girl and join the ushers while she joins the bridesmaids.

Trainbearers and pages are more prevalent at European weddings (possibly because kids are still seen and not heard in other cultures) than they are in America. Just try to get a five- or seven-year-old boy—who'd rather play hockey than go to the wedding at all—to hold a train, a veil, or anything else for more than five minutes. If I were you, I wouldn't risk it.

10 · Dressing for the Wedding

Dressing the Bride

I can't pinpoint what it is about wedding dresses that causes most women to react in a peculiar emotional way. Some will look away longingly and describe the dress of their dreams as an elaborate historic costume, like the ball gowns worn by romantic heroines during the nineteenth century. Others simply want to distinguish themselves classically and traditionally, choosing instead the signature look of hand-clipped laces, pearl beading, and a chapel-length train. And then there are women who, for reasons of taste or embarrassment, reject the concept of a wedding dress altogether. Their idea—a beautifully tailored suit or simple dress that can be worn again and again.

Regardless of how diverse the fashion, sophistication, and styling may be, the wedding dress is rarely a matter of indifference. It has been known to prompt the kind of passionate single-mindedness that, if sustained throughout a marriage, could destroy a relationship in a matter of weeks. Brides may be ambivalent about whether to offer a salad course at the reception, but they'll fight, cajole, and persuade even the most resistant salesperson to change the sleeve from a short cap to a full bishop.

I suppose that a lot of sophisticated brides think it foolish and unbecoming to wear a traditional white gown with all the accouterments of schoolgirl innocence. Ironically, the color white as a symbol of virgin purity was popularized in sixteenth-century England (quite a new phenomenon by historical standards) when the not-so-pure Henry VIII was on the throne. All those sweet young things made their fashion statement, but white didn't actually catch on for weddings until the next century, and still it was an idea that was considered déclassé and eccentric in some circles. But then, television, *Vogue,* and Eugenia Sheppard weren't around to drive the message home. Eventually, wedding white, and all the attendant etiquette, became acceptable—even mandatory—in American society. And with it came the wedding-dress industry, the bridal magazines, and the catering palaces.

When the women's movement began more than a decade ago, bras were burned along with other symbols of sexual subservience. The white wedding dress—with all its implications of virginity and obedience to the husband—lost favor among feminists, and it has only recently been reinstated by that elite group as a valid fashion choice.

Consider my friend Martha, recently married for the first time at the age of thirty-eight. A successful businesswoman, Martha bought an exclusive hand-painted chiffon dress by a European designer. But about two weeks before her wedding, she mentioned that she thought she'd be too hot in that dress, and what did I think about it all. It was clear that Martha wanted to look like a bride rather than a guest at her nuptial celebration. So, with the help of a talented buyer at a prominent New York store, Martha was outfitted in one day with a stunning three-piece silk and lace bride's dress.

Another surprise was Carol, a flamboyant fashion editor who helped popularize counterculture clothes. I was sure that Carol would want a space-age wedding jump suit designed in silver polyurethane by Thierry Mugler. Instead, she chose a totally traditional dress and train of silk crepe de chine, Alençon lace, and pearl beading. True, she wore firehouse red stockings, for as she put it in an article for the *New York Times,* "I couldn't resist adding a visual wink to all that bridal white."

Even though the press has accurately reported a growing return to the traditions of the formal white wedding, there is overwhelming evidence that only a little more than half of all brides wear traditional dresses, the greater percentage being among women who are marrying for the first time. The rest choose what are called informal looks, which range from elaborate wedding suits to off-the-rack dresses. Either way, brides need information before plunking down their money.

The Wedding Dress Business

The wedding dress business still deals predominantly in "special orders," which means that a bride tries on and selects from among samples, and the store orders the dress in her size (with any modifications); then the bride has alteration fittings and eventually gets to take the dress home. All of this takes an average of four months to accomplish.

The process begins with a designer's idea of fashion, tempered by traditional precedent and last year's sales figures. Twice each year, approximately seventy-five wedding dress houses design fashion collections—one for the spring market, one for the fall—and present them to buyers from all over the country at either the New York showrooms or the regional showrooms in Dallas, Chicago, Atlanta, or Los Angeles. Within the collections, different "lines" are developed and might include special dresses for petites and large sizes, high couture, middle-range traditional and contemporary styles, informal boutique, dresses for second weddings, dresses for bridesmaids and flower girls, and headpieces and veils.

Even before "market" opens, some dresses have been purchased by the retailer, sight unseen, through advertising promotions in bridal magazines. Other styles will be selected during market in accordance with the store's buying budget. About three months after market, the samples are delivered to the local stores, and they are often presented to brides in the form of advertising or even live fashion shows. The samples that are purchased provide the manufacturer with a "cutting ticket" of, say, five hundred units for one moderately priced dress. If the dress is "hot," it might reorder at an average of ten to every sample sold.

This process of manufacturing is really an old-fashioned couturier concept which still appeals to aristocratic ladies of leisure who have the time and money to invest in their wardrobes. Bridal shops, like their couture counterparts, could not make available a $1,500 dress in a variety of sizes without courting financial ruin. The message is, of course, that brides with a passion for luxury and high styling must order their dresses well in advance of their weddings.

This does not mean that a store won't bend over backward for a bride who has barely a month to get it together. Some bridal specialty shops stock informal looks, sell couture samples when necessary, and have been known to successfully pressure manufacturers to service brides who need dresses in two weeks. Some large-volume retailers do stock formal dresses in sizes, and they promise three-day delivery on some styles. Needless to say, these dresses are not cut of pure silk and do not feature hand-clipped French laces and hand-sewn seed pearls. They are instead polyester dresses with domestic laces that are "bonded" to the fabric, and the pearls, if they exist, are pasted on. With it all, the price is right, and for some, the timing is perfect.

Some major department stores, such as Bloomingdale's and Macy's, dropped their bridal operations in order to accommodate what they perceived as the high-volume, high-turnover, limited-inventory sportswear business, which is claimed to be the most lucrative of all fashion departments in any store. Recently, with such stores as Saks Fifth Avenue, Neiman-Marcus, and Henri Bendel producing record profits in their bridal shops, some drop-outs are reconsidering their position on wedding wear.

But for now, if you've always wanted to be a Bloomingdale's bride, you're stuck with trying to find something suitable from the dress racks. One risk is obvious—a guest might show up in the same style and spoil your day. A case in point is the bride who purchased an Albert Nipon voile dress, white with pale lilac flowers, trimmed in Val lace. The first gasp came from the friend who happened to be wearing the same dress. The second came from the bride herself, who did indeed surprise her guests by what she wore. Still, Albert Nipon makes the kind of pretty dress that appeals to sophisticated brides who want a small wedding. So does Gunne Sax for juniors. And, if sportswear designers are in the mood, you might find a handkerchief linen Victorian skirt and blouse by Ralph Lauren, a delicately printed silk crepe de chine wrap dress by Calvin Klein, even a white linen suit by Perry Ellis.

In my experience, even within the informal ready-to-wear area of suits and street-length dresses, no one gives better value and styling than such bridal designers as Priscilla of Boston, Galina, Ron LoVece, Bridal Couture, Paula Varsalona, Phyllis Bianchi, et al. The problem is that these dresses can't be charged and taken home, for they're still purchased as special orders.

If you want an antique wedding dress, you'll pay for the age and exclusivity (anywhere from $1,000 to $5,000), just as you would for a nineteenth-century English pine armoire. If you buy an old dress, beware. It may fall apart before you walk down the aisle. If, however, the dress has been remade or fashioned anew from old lace, it can be absolutely fabulous. Some antique dress houses—such as Country Elegance in California, Jeanne's Fantasia, and Pat Kerr—will incorporate your own old lace into the dress or headpiece. You'll still have to handle it with care, avoiding the obvious pitfalls of a roller disco reception.

Sewing, Borrowing, Renting

If you're really a good seamstress, go ahead and try a simple laceless dress, but if you're going for hand-clipped lace, pearl or crystal beading, tucking, fagoting, or other expert embroidery or sewing techniques, don't do it. You'll probably wind up with a dress that looks homemade, a staggering material and labor cost (if you value your time), and wounds to your hands and fingernails that might shock him when he puts the ring on your finger.

Borrowing a friend's dress is tacky. Borrowing your sister's is suspicious. Wearing your mother's or grandmother's is fine.

We seem to have a double standard about renting wedding clothes. For the groom, it's terrific. For the bride, it's taboo. I suppose you could say it all goes back to the purity of the wedding dress, but my hunch is that most women simply reject the idea of renting clothes for any occasion, let alone their own weddings. The fur rental business, for example, has died out—partly because of the availability of inexpensive fake and fun furs, but mostly because it's a phony claim of status to wear something you don't own. And even though most wedding dresses—even the elaborate ones—can be cleaned, too much comes out in the wash because of their fragility.

Hats, Headpieces, and Veils

More than anything else, it's the hat, veil, or wreath of flowers that makes a bride a bride. Even more than the dress, the train, the tiny buttons, or the exotic fabrics and laces, the way you top it off makes the real difference. Think about the best supportive look for the dress you've bought, the practicality of that choice in relation to your religious ceremony, and the mobility and ease that the headpiece offers during the reception (unless you decide to change clothes for that part of the wedding).

The headpiece and veil or the mantilla are the truly traditional choices, and they are what look best with classic dresses. Most traditional headpieces start with a buckram or horsehair cap which is then covered with fabric, lace, or silk flowers. A veil is attached, either plain edged, roll edged, or lace edged. When the cap and veil are trimmed with the same lace, it is known as a mantilla. Usually the lace trimming matches the lace on the wedding dress itself, but sometimes an alternative embroidery is selected.

Veiling. Most illusion veiling is made of nylon, although silk is used by fine bridal and headpiece designers. The veiling is made of little cell-like holes. The smaller those holes, the better the veil. Veils come in a variety of lengths and shapes, and they can be doubled, tripled, or quadrupled in thickness. They can be embroidered with lace edging to create a mantilla effect; they can feature a blusher or face veil that's pushed back after the ceremony; they can even be ordered in pale colors. Sometimes a chapel-length veil will be worn with a floor-length dress to give the effect of a train.

Some wedding hats, especially the small, chic pillbox types, are trimmed with illusion veiling, but more often, Russian veiling is used. Russian veiling has wide diamond-cut holes, knotted at each connection. The veiling itself has more body than illusion and often covers just the eyes. It can be fashioned into a bow and streamers for another effect, and it also comes in colors.

Wide-brimmed hats. Depending on the lace used, these hats are dramatic and often expensive. They are perfect for garden weddings, but can be pretentious at an indoor ceremony and reception. The biggest complaint I have heard about the wide-brimmed hat is this: unless the bride's face is lighted perfectly with artificial illumination, the brim will cut off the natural supply of light and darken the image in a photograph. If you choose to wear a wide-brimmed hat, be sure your photographer shoots at the right angle and fills or reflects the necessary light onto your face. Smart bridal milliners, aware of the problem, are trimming their hats with detachable silk flowers that can be pinned to the hair when the hat is removed for the reception.

Small hats. From toques to cloches to turbans, tams, and pillboxes, wedding hats come in all shapes and sizes. Most of the more sophisticated varieties feature a touch of Russian veiling rather than yards of illusion, and they complement the notion of a street-length, ballet-length, or floor-length dress or suit. The beauty of the small hat is that it usually works well with short or long hair. (Long hair is often rolled or swept up to accent the look of the hat.) And brides like the fact that small hats don't interfere with dancing, kissing, or photo lighting.

Wreaths and floral headpieces. These styles can be made with silk flowers (with touches of color, if desired), lace flowers, pearl rosettes, jewels and crystals, or any combination of these materials. Such headpieces are growing in popularity because the veil can be detached later for the reception.

Yes, you can have your florist design a wreath of fresh flowers, but after two hours they'll probably look as wilted as your caterer. Besides, they can't really be preserved or pressed. If you like the idea of delicately scented fresh flowers such as freesias, add them, in small clusters, to your hat or headpiece. If they discolor or wilt, you haven't lost everything.

Accessories

Like so many things about weddings, accessories for brides and attendants can really be overdone. Why would anyone have bridesmaids walk down a church aisle holding parasols? Surely the light reflected through the stained glass is not that harsh. Even antique or lace fans, which have become popular, are a little out of place at a winter wedding. Still, the right accessories can make the look of your wedding more cohesive, more exciting, and more finished.

Open necklines, such as the sweetheart, Queen Anne's, the scoop neck, or off-the-shoulder can be enhanced with a strand of pearls, a locket, or a diamond-studded gold chain. Pearl or diamond earrings can also be attractive, especially with small-brimmed hats.

Remember that a ring will probably be placed on your finger, so if you're wearing lace gloves, remove both of them and hand them to your maid of honor or a bridesmaid. Lace gauntlets are also available, usually made by dress designers to go with their short-sleeved styles. Whether you carry flowers, a fan, a prayer book, or an old lace handkerchief, make sure it doesn't look like a theatrical prop and that it doesn't overwhelm the proportion of your dress.

Stockings can be pale ivory or sheer white, patterned or embroidered if you like. And your shoes should be comfortable as well as stylish. Strappy sandals in silk-satin or peau de soie are great for spring and summer; pumps work all year round.

If your wedding and reception have a Western flavor, you can go all the way with a straw stetson hat, white cowboy boots, even a lace holster to hold a posy of flowers. If Victoriana is your theme, you can wear a lace boater hat, carry a walking stick wrapped with ribbons and flowers, and strut around in turn-of-the-century lace pumps. But watch the theatrics for a theme wedding lest it look like a scene from *Hello, Dolly.*

Facts and Figures

Even though the average bride spends between $500 and $600 for her wedding dress, she can go as low as $150 or as high as $7,000, and by the time she's through with a headpiece and all the accessories, she's in for a relatively large sum of money. Whether you spend a lot or not, you should know the value of the materials and the workmanship in your dress. The laces and fabrics in the following charts represent the most commonly used materials. They are listed from top to bottom according to their cost.

Most manufacturers, in accordance with consumer laws, indicate fabric content and give cleaning instructions. But not all the trims, laces, and linings will be identified. Whether the lace is hand- or machine-made, almost all the fine imports have their domestic counterparts. Some can pass as good reproductions. Some you wouldn't choose for kitchen curtains. There are nylon and rayon sheer fabrics that are called organza, but few have the "denier" (weight) of the real thing. You'll know when you feel it. Trust your instincts.

Tips on Buying a Wedding Dress

1. Look through the bridal magazines to get an overview of the designs available.
2. Bring a friend, your mother, or himself with you (unless you're absolutely secure about your fashion image). Said one bride: "I wouldn't think of buying my wedding suit without Bob's okay. He cares more about what I wear than I do."
3. If you want a formal dress, start to shop at least six months in advance of the wedding. (Some bridal specialty salons request appointments so that they can spend time showing you all the available dresses from behind the closet doors.)
4. Have a budget in mind, and tell the salesperson to show you dresses within it.
5. Bring or wear comfortable shoes in the same heel height you'll wear for the wedding.
6. Even if you don't normally wear one, bring a bra (preferably strapless), so you can get a better fit.
7. Wear your hair in the style you'll want at the wedding, or bring bobby pins so you can experiment with a style that will be compatible with your headpiece or hat.

Laces and Embroideries

Type	Description	Notes
Brussels lace (Belgium)	Delicate, lightweight, subtle patterns.	A dress made completely of unbeaded Brussels lace could cost $5,000 or more. Limited availability.
Alençon lace (France)	Corded or reembroidered design, connected by net ground. Floral, paisley patterns.	Expensive. Usually used to embroider bodices, hems. If generously appliquéd on fine fabric, could cost $1,500 or more, without beading.
Venise lace (Italy)	Guipure type, connected by "bride." Heavy feel, made of linen or cotton. Leaf, floral patterns.	Looks best in pure white, used primarily in spring or summer. As trimming on fine fabric, can cost $600 or more.
Chantilly lace (France)	The real stuff is soft and fragile in weblike patterns.	Limited availability. For a complete dress, could cost around $3,000.
Embroidered organza (Switzerland)	Patterns of dimensional flowers with rolled edges, often tinted in soft colors.	Summer look. Complete dress, around $1,000.
Silk flowers (France)	Handmade, hand-dyed, hand-rolled. Beautiful colors.	Used by couture designers as trimming on fine fabrics. For bodice and hem accents, $800 to $1,000.
Schiffli embroidery (United States)	Fine, delicate patterns, similar to Brussels lace.	The best is made from a cotton and polyester fiber base. Dresses trimmed at bodices and skirts on good fabrics, around $500.

8. Find out before depositing any money what the store's cancellation policy is; how much they charge for special alterations (normal fittings are usually included in the price); and how soon you might expect delivery.

9. If you're buying an expensive couture dress, you can often order (and pay for) changes in the styling. You may want zippers replaced with tiny covered buttons, sleeves changed from short to long, or a train made longer or shorter.

Spring and Summer Fabrics

Type	Description	Notes
Silk organza (France)	Sheer, crisp texture. Feminine appeal.	Uncommon because it wrinkles easily. Expensive.
Poly-silk organza (Japan)	The most commonly used among better design houses. Retains sheer, crisp texture.	Look for double-layer construction. With minimum trimming would cost $600.
Poly-organza (Japan)	Easily appliquéd, good texture, wrinkle free.	Look for double-layer construction. With minimum trimming, would cost $500.
Silk chiffon (Italy, France)	Tissue weight, floaty, sheer.	Expensive. Will stretch unevenly—must be left to hang before sewing. Should have multilayers for proper effect. Never hang before wearing.
Poly-silk chiffon	Good alternative.	Never hang before wearing. Should be laid flat, pressed with care. Without trimming, costs anywhere from $300 to $500.
Poly-chiffon (also known as Italian chiffon)	Judge for yourself. Can be too "heavy" in comparison to others.	Same as above, but a little less expensive.
Crepe—poly or rayon	Soft, fluid. Can be tucked, fagoted.	Moderate price, depending on trim.
Voile (cotton/poly blend)	Lightweight, summery, often tucked, smocked, gathered, appliquéd.	Less expensive, pretty, youthful. Good for informal looks. Usually appliquéd with domestic laces or embroideries. Average cost of complete dress, around $300.
Linen (blend)	Stiffer fabric, used for tailored shapes and suits.	More common for bridesmaids. Costs vary with construction and design.
Batistes, eyelets, piqués (mostly blends of cotton/poly)	Summery, usually pure white. Detail is in fabric rather than trim.	Inexpensive, feminine, pretty. Less formal. Cost, from $200 to $400.

10. When the salesperson takes your measurements, be sure it is done properly. (See the chart below.)

11. Remember that the shape of the skirt will change (and become a bit shorter) if you wear full petticoats. If your dress needs that fullness, buy the petticoat and include it in the budgeted cost of your wedding dress.

12. If you're lucky enough to be a size 8 or 10, you may be able to buy a sample at discount. The dress might be from a past season; it may need cleaning or repair; it may be perfect. Don't hesitate to ask to see these samples. At the very least, you'll be able to compare the relative costs of an existing dress or a special-order item.

13. Don't turn into an anoretic or a compulsive eater before your wedding. Your dress just won't fit.

The following size chart is what designer Ron LoVece recommends to stores. LoVece notes that his standard sample length is 57 inches from hollow to hem, and his underarm sleeve length is 18 inches.

Measurement Chart

Size	4	6	8	10	12	14	16	18	20
Bust	32	33	34	35	36	37½	39	41	43
Waist	22	23	24	25	26	27½	29	31	33
Hips	32	33	34	35	36	37½	39	41	43

When ordering dresses other than standard sizes, please use following measurements:

Bodice length: Hollow of neck to empire seam or waist seam.

Skirt length: From empire or waist seam to finished hem or lowest point of lace scallop.

Sleeve length: From underarm seam to wrist hem.

Length of princess line dresses: From hollow of neck to finished hem or lowest point of lace scallop.

Beauty and the Bride

Health. As always, beauty starts with a healthy body (good skin and hair follow), and that means a regular program of exercise, good food, and a reasonable amount of sleep. Don't take up hang gliding; just continue your regular tennis game. It sounds easy, but the topsy-turvy prewedding schedule may throw your whole routine out of whack. If you've planned well and learned how to say no to some of the parties and celebrations, you'll keep the control you need to stay fit. The inevitable advice, "everything in moderation," might be predictable, but it is never more appropriate than now.

1. Lower your intake of caffeine.
2. Cut down on drinking and smoking.
3. Supplement your diet with stress vitamins.
4. Unless your sex life with your husband-to-be is already established, see a gynecologist to decide on a suitable method of birth control and to make sure you're in good physical shape. *Caution:* Do not try an IUD a week before the wedding. Some women react badly. If you're one of them, you'll be miserable.
5. If you can do it, take at least two days off from work before

Nonseasonal Fabrics

Type	Description	Notes
Taffeta (silk or silk/poly blend)	Tissue quality. Lightweight, opaque.	Used by couture designers. Expensive. Often has all-lace bodice and sleeves. $800 and up.
Tulle (nylon)	Fairy princess appeal. Floaty, pretty.	Should have lots of layers in full skirt. Ball gown bodice construction. With silk flower trim, anywhere from $800 to $1,600.
English net	Fine cotton netting, traditional wedding dress fabric. Sheer, but with body.	Expensive. Usually appliquéd with Alençon lace. $1,000 and up.
Jersey (almost exclusively blended fabrics)	Soft, fluid. Varies in quality and feel. Some are satin finished, some are matte. You'll know the quality when you feel it.	Difficult to appliqué. Usually the bodice is lace, the skirt is plain. Dresses fall within $200–$500 range.

Fall and Winter Fabrics

Type	Description	Notes
Silk-faced satin	Beautiful finish, heavyweight, traditional.	Used by couture designers. Expensive. Is appliquéd with finest laces. Cost, $1,000 and up.
Faille, either pure silk or poly blend	Stiff, full-bodied, line-textured fabric.	Used by couture designers. Usually tailored in basic construction. About $500 or up.
Peau de soie (blended)	Matte finished; lightweight but holds shape.	It used to be pure silk. But even the blend is expensive. Figure $600 and up with lace embroidery.
Velvet (cotton)	Pile finish, soft matte look.	Usually constructed as basic with braiding or piping. $400 and up.
Velvet (nylon)	Forget it. Looks and feels junky.	Used by volume producers. Even this will cost upwards of $200.
Brocades, damasks, jacquards, other novelty fabrics	The pattern is embossed in the fabric. The quality depends on the fiber content.	Usually designed in tailored looks. Prices depend on styling.
Rayon satin	Shiny finish, weight varies. Seams, if unfinished, can easily ravel.	Used by moderate-priced manufacturers. Trimmed with traditional laces. Figure $300 and up.
Crepe de chine (polyester)	Blouse-weight quality. Soft, floaty.	Good for informals. Moderate prices, depending on trim.

the wedding. Do nothing except pamper yourself. Try a sauna and massage, or swim at the Y each day.

6. Don't try to get a Coppertone tan the day before your wedding. If you're tempted, see a rerun of *The Heartbreak Kid.*

7. If you are thinking about embarking on a new beauty program of facial cleansing, depilatory waxing, or electrolysis, do it well in advance of the wedding. Your skin might break out as a result of this treatment.

Makeup. Surrounded by a sea of white, your makeup has to look terrific—and that means a little more color. Without it, you could be a washout. That's not to say you should give up your natural good looks for false eyelashes and Miss Piggy's rouge. Professional makeup artists could be your best source for providing perfect wedding makeup. Try them out in advance, of course, and keep a written record of what they used. If you decide to book them for your wedding, you can jog their memories, product for product, eyelash for eyelash.

If you prefer an independent approach, go to a department store makeup counter, have your makeup done, and buy the products so you can duplicate the look at home. Bear in mind that natural daylight and incandescent evening light affect makeup differently. For daytime weddings, less intense coloration is recommended. For evening, richer, deeper tones are best. Here's what the experts suggest:

1. Emphasize the eyes with subtle brown or gray shadows. Brush-on or cream shadows are best, but a delicate pencil could be used to shade the underlid.
2. Carefully apply mascara to both top and bottom lashes to widen and highlight the eyes.
3. If you don't use a makeup base, be sure to use a moisturizer to achieve a glowing and even complexion.
4. Toners and blushers should be applied to emphasize cheekbones and add color and vitality to your face. If you're wearing a dress with an open neckline, be sure to carefully blush and blend the neck and collar area.
5. Lipstick should be vivid without appearing garish or harsh. Pencil outlines filled in with brushstroke creams give the best results. Finish it off with a subtle gloss.
6. Maintain a matte finish with a buff of baby powder.
7. Ask a friend (not a bridesmaid or your mother) to carry your makeup for you. You'll want to retouch it before the photos are taken.

Hair. Want a permanent? A henna dye? Tipping, streaking, cold waving, even a new haircut? Do it at least 2 weeks before the wedding. Otherwise, work with what you've got and make it fabulous. Long, straight hair might look terrific swinging at a disco, but that sporty look will be out of place with a wedding dress and veil. Whether it's straight or curly, long hair can ruin the proportion of a hat, a mantilla, or a high-necked dress. Consider instead a simple chignon, hair roll, or Gibson girl topknot. If you're wearing a wreath and veil, long crimped hair could be romantic and lovely, as gentle as a midsummer night's dream.

Short hair should be trimmed a week before the wedding; it looks terrific with the chic pillboxes and narrow-brimmed hats. Most beauty salons will happily take wedding party appointments on the day of the wedding, and some, for a special fee, will be available to come to your home. Do not expect one individual to perform miracles on you, your six bridesmaids, and your mother in two hours. Discuss it all in advance (including the fee), and find out if he or she wants you to wash and set your hair yourself, provide hot rollers, a curling iron, or any other tool of hair torture.

Most headpieces have a comb attached to the inside of the frame. Take a lock of your hair at the point you want the headpiece secured. Make a pin curl and put in two bobby pins in the shape of an X. Put the comb into the X, and it will stay on your head until you remove it. If no comb is provided with the headpiece, use white bobby pins, pushed through the lace trimming and into the hair.

Dressing the Groom

Choosing clothes for the groom used to be simple. The classic stroller and striped trousers for a formal morning wedding; the cutaway for the afternoon; the black-tie tuxedo or white tie and tails for evening. Then came powder blue and polyester, the very ruffled shirt, and a kind of Las Vegas entertainer fashion look. The reason for the trend? Formalwear manufacturers wanted antitraditionalists to rent wedding attire. The concept worked.

Throughout the 1970s, the "formal suit," in all its wash and wear colors, created a new and successful market in the formalwear industry. And even though the colors have been neutralized for the eighties (tans, champagnes, ecrus, grays), the formal suit, so familiar with its single- or double-breasted jacket, peaked lapels or shawl collar, single or double vents, and matching trousers, is here to stay.

Still, there are men who shun the whole idea of dressing up in "monkey suits," preferring their favorite garb from Brooks Brothers. It is this man who challenges the manufacturer most. He won't follow the old rules; he won't be compromised by the new. Surely there's one tactic that can't fail—and that's the designer label. The marketing strategy, pitched to prom kings and grooms alike, leaves no room for resistance. The method: sell the designer name to the bride through the magazines, and the groom will capitulate.

Actually, these designer suits—which include Bill Blass for After Six, Yves St. Laurent, Pierre Cardin for Lord West, and John Weitz for Palm Beach—are a cut above the rest in both fabric and tailoring. They are close to the traditional attire of striped trousers, ascots, cutaways, and the like, but are upgraded in styling.

For a garden wedding, nothing is more attractive than a navy blue blazer and white or gray flannel trousers. Beige, gray, or white linen dress suits are also appropriate, along with dark navy blue gabardine for informal or semiformal summer weddings. And for fall or winter, dark gray or blue flannel, serge, or cashmere is elegant and attractive.

The only formal wedding costume worth buying is the tuxedo. "Black tie" can be worn for any formal evening occasion and is often a requested form of dress at parties, dinners, and balls. (Etiquette dictates, by the way, that the evening officially begins at 6:00 P.M.) What happens when the style goes out of fashion? Here's a story told by a member of the class of '59: "I hadn't seen them for 20 years, and I wanted to impress them with my success and status. I even bought a new tuxedo for the occasion. The dark paneled walls and dim lights made it hard to see at first, but slowly it dawned on me that the men I admired most in that room owned their tuxedoes 20 years ago, and they were secure enough to wear them now. They looked like the gentlemen they truly were. I looked and felt like an advertisement in *Gentlemen's Quarterly*."

In a recent issue of *Esquire,* Vincent Boucher advised, "The best tuxedo is the tuxedo you own. Even if your formal appearances are limited to a handful of events each season, it's worthwhile in terms of time, money, and your own image to wear well-fitting evening clothes."

The average tuxedo costs about $250, not including accessories. The average rental is around $50, and includes all accessories except for shoes and socks.

Accessories for the Groom

If the groom wants to be noticed, too, he can wear a gray top hat with his cutaway, a black top hat with tails, or a dramatic cape with his white-tie evening look. One groom did it, but made the mistake of donning white gloves. Everyone wondered if there was a rabbit in his hat.

Cummerbunds are handsome additions to tuxedoes. They can also be rented with those formal suits and seem to help. But vests (unlike traditional waistcoats that coordinate with the classics) fight the idea of formality and turn the look into a Wall Street knock-off.

If the groom is buying his own tuxedo, he will need a beautiful set of studs and cuff links to go with it. A classic choice is onyx set in gold. You might want to buy these for him. For shirts, look for flat pleating rather than ruffles, although some of the ruffles can be subtle and handsome. For wing collar shirts, try to have him buy a real bow tie that he or you can knot to perfection. If he wants the convenience of a hook and eye, make sure the hardware is hidden.

Patent leather pumps are classic, but some men can't adjust to grosgrain bows. Any highly polished black dress shoe will do. Oh, what the hell, even a Gucci loafer's okay.

I like boutonnieres more than handkerchiefs for weddings. If the ushers wear carnations, the groom can have a rose. If they wear roses, he can have a sprig of lily of the valley. It's all part of being singled out as the man of the hour.

What to Wear for Your Kind of Wedding

Informal (day or evening)	Blazer or business suit
Semiformal (daytime)	Blazer or business suit; stroller with striped trousers; or simple formal suit
Semiformal (evening)	Dark business suit; tuxedo; or formal suit
Formal (morning)	Stroller with striped trousers; or formal suit
Formal (afternoon)	Cutaway with wing collar and ascot; or formal suit
Formal (evening)	Tuxedo; or formal suit
Ultraformal (evening)	White tie and tails

Dressing the Bridesmaids

Like wedding dresses, bridesmaid dresses are special ordered to accommodate the variety of sizes and shapes of your attendants. Even if you're paying for your bridesmaids' dresses, you can't afford to be the kind of fashion dictator who ignores the personal style and taste of your friends. Yes, you can choose the color, but it shouldn't be Day-Glo chartreuse. Yes, you can select the style, but it should flatter all the figures in the wedding party. And you shouldn't expect your friends to spend two hundred dollars on an outfit they'll wear only once. Knowing all this, bridesmaid designers do indeed try to cater to both the practical and fashionable sides of weddings.

Typically, bridesmaid dresses are one-piece costumes in chiffon, voile, jersey, point d'esprit, or rayon sheer over taffeta. They're often trimmed with cotton or Venise lace or yoked with delicate embroidery. The colors are as predictable as the styling—soft pastels for warm weather, jewel colors for cold.

There's no doubt that these traditional dresses can be pretty and easily coordinated with a bride's own look, but when all is said and done, the bridesmaid is left with an $80 to $100 dress that will sit in her closet forever. That's a pretty big investment for any woman who would prefer to buy a dress she could wear more than once.

Manufacturers have responded to the cry for multipurpose bridesmaid clothing without, in most cases, compromising the effect down the aisle. The styling device used most often is the sexy bodice covered with a demure jacket, shawl, or cape. You can, for example, buy a revealing halter top floor-length jersey dress with a sheer chiffon blouson jacket that is outlined in lace. After the wedding, the skirt can be shortened and worn at discos or cocktail parties.

Another "hot" item for bridesmaids is the dress-over-skirt. The ceremonial look is that of a floor-length tiered skirt, but the underlayer, fashioned with an elasticized waist, is removable, leaving you with a simple street-length dress. Separates—blouses and skirts—are also part of the picture and clearly live an independent life.

If you can't imagine dressing your friends in polyester jersey or chiffon rather than the silk they're used to wearing for special occasions, you're stuck with searching through the racks of ready-to-wear formals for four or five dresses in different sizes that have some semblance of coordination. One bride came up with an inventive solution when she discovered a line of silk coordinates, sized small, medium, and large. The designer developed a moderate-priced line which included tops, jackets, skirts, and trousers in a selection of colors that mixed and matched beautifully. The bride, knowing that even a maid in silk pajamas would look right at her wedding, simply advised her four friends to buy whatever look appealed to them. Another bride, who wanted all her sisters dressed alike, hired a dressmaker and provided her with peach silk crepe de chine and a photograph from the pages of *Vogue*.

If you prefer just one friend to all the sisters from Gamma Omega Chi, none of the above applies. She'll either buy a new dress or wear an old favorite that won't fight with your wedding concept. If two good friends are involved, you can suggest that one wear a print, the other a solid color, or that they absolve you of the responsibility and coordinate their own looks.

Tips for Dressing the Bridesmaids

1. Rainbow weddings—each bridesmaid in a different pastel color—are passé.
2. You might try having your maid or matron of honor wear a dress that subtly sets her apart from the bridesmaids.
3. The dyed-to-match pump is a waste of money. A strappy sandal in metallics, dyed snakeskin, or bicolored silk might cost more than a cheap pump, but it will serve the buyer for a longer time.
4. Parasols and picture hats are expensive and unnecessary.
5. Haircombs adorned with fabric flowers, jewels, or pearls make terrific headpieces that can be worn again.

In all, sometimes you save money by spending more.

Dressing the Children

Your or his children can be dressed up in the kind of clothes that fit the style and size of your wedding. You can rationalize spending sixty dollars or more for your five-year-old girl, even though there's no future in it. The dress will take a permanent backseat to her designer jeans, and by the time she's ready to haul it out for a special holiday, she'll have outgrown it. Still, your own kids need to feel as important as possible on this day, and they deserve this kind of attention. If the child or children you've selected as flower girls or ring bearers are not your own, you should pay for their costumes. Unless the parents are truly wealthy and offer to pay for the clothes in a very convincing way, you should bear the costs.

For little girls, there are charming dresses, often designed by bridesmaid manufacturers to coordinate with the big girls. A little girl will usually take it all very seriously, acting particularly grown up and charming. But even a nonsexist little boy will probably be more reticent, especially if you want to dress him in cute shorts, knee socks, and a ruffled shirt. The alternative is to rent a miniature version of the groomsmen's suits. For a boy of 8 years or older, the "little man" idea might work. My advice is to let him wear a classic blazer and flannels, and pin a flower in his lapel.

Dressing the Groomsmen

The groom's wedding suit will determine what the best man and ushers will wear. Traditionally, all are dressed alike, but with the advent of coordinated formal suits, grooms and best men can dress similarly but differently from the ushers. The groom can wear a double-breasted jacket while the others go single. Or he can have baby blue tails while the rest settle for sack coats. If a groom must outshine his friends, it is usually best to do so with accessories, such as a cummerbund, a hat, or gloves.

Like bridesmaids, groomsmen pay for their own wedding clothes. If your friends are scattered in different cities, get their sizes, and order the suits from a formalwear rental shop. Check in advance with the salesperson about how to measure for accurate sizes. All the alterations, such as cuffing trousers from inseam measurements, will be done in advance, but it is still best to have a final fitting. This can be done as late as the day before the wedding.

If the wedding is black tie and some of the groomsmen own tuxedoes, they should wear them, even though the styles won't be identical. Costs vary with the item being rented, but groomsmen can expect to pay between $45 and $60 for their outfits.

Both fathers can wear wedding attire to maintain the consistent look of the wedding party. This is especially true of the bride's father, who may walk her down the aisle. Nevertheless, dark business suits will suffice. And both men would wear boutonnieres to distinguish them from the guests.

If no formal clothes are required, ushers and fathers should be dressed similarly, but not identically. Don't expect anyone to buy a double-breasted navy blue blazer when they already own one that's single breasted. You can request gray flannels, but don't insist that they all be pleated or cuffed. If the word is to wear a dark business suit, some will be navy blue, others charcoal gray. It doesn't matter if they're different.

Mothers and Other VIPs

Mothers don't have to buy new dresses unless they want to. For almost any daytime wedding a street-length dressy dress or suit is fine. Long dresses are okay if it's really formal, but that length is preferred for evening. The bride's mother, according to old rules, has the right to choose the style and color of her dress, and only then can the groom's mother select a compatible alternative. The idea was that his family could not outshine yours. If your mother declared short, *she* wouldn't dare show up in a floor-length Bill Blass. This old rule, instituted to protect the bride's mother against one-upmanship, seems as primitive as a car without power steering. And it shouldn't be invoked if all the parents are participating equally.

Among civilized people, a simple conversation will take place resulting in an agreement about what to wear when the kids get married. And so what if both like pearl pink and wear it that day? Most people will think it was planned.

Grandmothers, godparents, great-aunts, and other VIPs will take their cues from you or your mother when you tell them how formal or informal the wedding will be.

Advice to Guests

If the invitation itself doesn't indicate the formality of the wedding, a guest should call the bride and find out. A bride will never forgive someone who outdresses her. And what I call the "new divorcée look" (more flesh than fabric) will raise eyebrows and maybe even Cain. On the flip side, a corduroy jump suit or anyone's designer jeans are just plain insulting, unless the couple specifies "ultracasual." Silk evening trousers are acceptable, but slacks and pantsuits are not.

I guess most people don't own evening clothes anymore. When they try to outfit themselves for a formal occasion, they give away their secret by some glaring fashion faux pas. An evening wedding during the fall or winter really tells the story. You spot it first at the church, where you see a woman clad in a floor-length formal topped with a hooded car coat. There's usually not an evening bag in sight, but, rather, the purses and oversized shoulder bags that only work with sport clothes.

I'm not advocating the purchase of a Fendi fur coat for the sake of the wedding. But a blanket shawl, evening sweater, or quilted satin jacket will at least add a touch of evening flair without breaking the bank. And men should brave the cold and leave the raincoats home, or take the cashmere toppers out of mothballs.

Little girls should wear dresses or pretty skirts and blouses with appropriate tights or anklets, and dress shoes. No sportswear, please. Boys should have jackets with trousers or suits with long or short pants. Even though they'll protest, they shouldn't wear running shoes.

11 · *Finishing Touches for the Wedding*

The Wedding Music

At a church or synagogue, whether you choose the Beatles, Bach, or both, your wedding music should be handled with care. Music sets the tone before the ceremony while people are being seated; it introduces you and your attendants during the processional; and it celebrates your marriage via the recessional. Too many false notes, and your wedding could be overshadowed or even trivialized by the selections. If your wedding is to be traditional, but not predictable, you may eschew Wagner's "Wedding March" from *Lohengrin* ("Here Comes the Bride") and Mendelssohn's "Wedding March" from *A Midsummer Night's Dream,* but you should avoid substituting selections by the Grateful Dead or the Rolling Stones. Wedding music, if properly chosen, will enhance the religious significance of your ceremony, not detract from it.

Some faiths forbid secular music, restricting the use of instruments other than their own church organ, and they have rules about vocalists, including Aunt Margaret singing "Ave Maria." It is customary to discuss your ideas with your clergyman first, then meet with the musical director (usually the organist) to finalize the selections. Although most of the rules concerning wedding music have been amended in favor of a liberal approach, some church officials will deny your request for contemporary selections, insisting that "I Love You Truly" is the only way to go. And even though the clergyman may be confusing his own tastes with church dogma, it is not in your best interest to start your own reform church movement. Try to reach a compromise by using his approved music for the ceremony itself, yours for the pre-wedding gathering period.

A couple married in a Greek Orthodox service found a perfect solution. While the guests were being seated, ballads by Paul McCartney, Joni Mitchell, Carole King, and James Taylor were played on the organ. The couple provided the sheet music, carefully avoiding songs that, when interpreted for the organ, would sound as if they belonged at an old-fashioned roller rink.

For their processional, Air from the *Water Music* suite by Handel was a perfect introduction to the elaborate ceremony that followed. The old-world liturgy called for the church cantor to sing Byzantine chants a cappella. And Beethoven's "Ode to Joy" from his Ninth Symphony was played for the recessional. Naturally, all the selections were approved by the priest, who later confided that he thought the music was beautifully balanced and presented. By the way, the bride and groom had the wit to pay an additional fee to the organist, who had agreed to run through all the selections during the wedding rehearsal.

For a home or garden wedding, a pianist, harpsichordist, violinist, classical guitarist, or string quartet can give just the right effect—a kind of spiritual intimacy to a fairly formal wedding. One of the prettiest garden weddings I can remember was hosted at a lovely Victorian house in the country. As people approached the house from the various entrances, strains of Bach or Mozart greeted them from the chamber music quartet positioned on the porch. The players looked like they came from Central Casting, their baroque features imitating the harpsichord, violins, and cello.

When the bride and her father descended the porch steps for the processional, Bach's "Jeso" (Jesus Joy of Man's Desiring) was played, and after the ceremony, "Adagio in A Minor" was the joyful recessional. Said the bride, "Our wedding ceremony deserved more than a group sing of 'Amazing Grace,' especially since the setting was so familiar and casual."

The advantages of a tape system may persuade you to forget about live music altogether. The space at a house or apartment may not be large enough to accommodate musicians and their instruments, and even if you manage to squeeze them in, the volume may be overwhelming. With tapes, you will have total control over the selections and timing, you'll save money, and you'll have a permanent record of your wedding music.

Don't try records. Your appointed disc jockey will be skipping around albums, trying to find the right cut, sending shivers up spines as the needle scratches its way in search of the perfect étude. If you don't own a tape deck or any stereo equipment, borrow or rent what you need. Tape the music you want to match your ceremony timetable. If guests are gathering for a half an hour or so before the ceremony begins, tape one side of a 90-minute cassette (or its equivalent in 8-track) for the prewedding music. Side two would begin with the processional, cut to a 10-second pause, then the recessional, followed by postceremony music.

Tips for Using Recorded Music

1. Good quality 90-minute cassettes will give you clear, undistorted sound. It's best not to go to 120 minutes. The tapes are thin and tend to break.
2. If your system is sophisticated enough, you can use your auxiliary jacks to record the ceremony even if another tape is running. Check the instructions or, even better, consult with a sound technician from a stereo shop or a local radio station.
3. If you're using this system in a garden or multiroom house, you may need to add additional speakers to the "B" jack in order to have balanced sound.
4. Before the wedding, test the system in the presence of the friend who will be in charge of it.

Selecting Classical Music

Record and tape libraries are good and inexpensive sources for listening to classical music before you make your selections. Some let you "check out," others make you play the music in soundproof booths or listen with earphones. Usually, a knowledgeable librarian will suggest certain symphonic excerpts and other works, but it is best to come armed with a list of possibilities.

If you like the idea, you might post a notice or call your local symphony orchestra, graduate school or conservatory of music, or classical instruction center and offer a consulting fee to any expert who agrees to help you. If you make the deal, that individual should be able to make recommendations and may even have the records or tapes available for you to hear.

In large cities, there are shops that specialize in classical, jazz, disco, and other kinds of recordings. The proprietor brings his own erudition to the merchandise and can probably be tapped for ideas. But don't take up an hour of his time without buying something.

If your local newspaper has a classical music reviewer or reporter, he or she may be willing to help. If no payment is requested or made, send a gift of flowers or wine.

The musical director at your church or synagogue has probably heard it all and could be the first and last word on the subject. Don't reject his or her ideas out of hand, since they may save you an enormous amount of time and effort.

The Wedding Flowers

Some churches restrict the use of flowers to the altar and pews only. Others let you decorate the chancel and windows as well. Obviously, the most elaborate floral arrangements should only be used for very formal weddings. Generally, all you need is some kind of arrangement at the altar. Talk to your florist about the size of each arrangement in relation to the proportions of the altar and church. Avoid anything that might look funereal like large sprays of gladiolas in fake white vases. You can coordinate these flowers with your overall color scheme, mixing dried, fresh, or silk ones if you like. You can be imaginative without creating the look of a convention hall flower show. If fire laws permit, for example, candlelight sconces or table displays are beautiful for evening ceremonies. Pews can be marked by ribbons or small posies of baby's breath and flowers.

If you want a hedge of greenery to cordon off part of the church, you can rent plants from a local nursery, but this is an expensive proposition and may not be worth it. One bride reported that after the dozen ficus trees were in place, the church still looked like a too-large church with an odd-looking row of ficus trees in the middle.

Most Jewish weddings call for a special arrangement of flowers decorating the *huppah,* or canopy, under which the couple stands for the ceremony. Originally, the *huppah* was made of silk or velvet cloth that was ringed at the edges and supported by four posts. In *The Jewish Wedding Book,* authors Lilly S. Routtenberg and Ruth R. Seldin say that the *huppah* "is a faint echo of the Jews' tribal heritage, perhaps symbolic of the 3rd legal form of marriage, cohabitation. In earliest times, the bride was led to the groom's tent or chamber, where the marriage was consummated."

It was probably another tradition, however, that gave rise to the idea of a *huppah* created entirely of flowers. In ancient times, a tree was planted for any child born, a tradition still practiced by some Jews. When a marriage took place, a branch from each tree would be joined to form a canopy. This custom has translated into the expensive and elaborate floral *huppah.* As one bride commented, "It's fine when you know the purpose and tradition—it's lousy when all you have is a two-hundred-dollar flower bill."

Tips for Saving Money on Flowers

1. For the altar arrangements, instead of cut flowers, use potted azaleas, gardenias, chrysanthemums, or other flowering perennials. They can be planted later in your own garden, given to the church as a "charitable contribution," or rented and returned to the nursery. If clusters of smaller flowering plants such as tulips or geraniums are more appropriate, you may need to build a platform to create the necessary levels.

2. Some florists recommend "sharing" altar arrangements with other brides who will be marrying either the same day or the next day. You can ask your clergyman if another wedding is scheduled and then contact the bride yourself. If she agrees, you may both have to compromise with colors and choices, but it may be worth it.

3. Pew markers can be simplified, too. A single rose laced in a tiny bunch of baby's breath or fern leaves is less expensive than a full floral spray. Silk flowers nestled in a bow of ribbon might cost more per unit, but they can make lovely permanent table arrangements later. Just make sure someone collects them after the ceremony.

4. A *huppah* can be trimmed with greenery interspersed with flowers rather than created entirely of flowers. Smilax or woven ivy can provide the garland, filled out with baby's breath or candytuft and dotted with roses or carnations.

5. Always work with seasonal flowers.

For a home or garden wedding, you can create an altar with the same kind of formal sprays or flowering plants, but if you want to be less elaborate, you can easily streamline the decorations by using pretty table arrangements or sconces. Most rooms have a decorating scheme, so be sure to choose flowers that don't fight with the pink and yellow chintz slipcovers. Clusters of glass bud vases with single stemmed flowers are pretty by day, and they can be offset with votive candles at night. Don't forget to put small arrangements in the bathrooms, or, if you prefer, scented candles.

Money savers. Tiny clay pots of begonias, impatiens, or other summer annuals will last and last. For spring, potted tulips or other bulb flowers are ideal. If you can't replant them yourself, give them to someone who can.

For a garden wedding, look around and find the perfect tree or flower bed, centrally located, to serve as the background for your ceremony. If the blooms are flourishing, there's no need to place standing arrangements or showier flowers in their path. And a delicate or majestic tree shouldn't be violated or decorated for the occasion. The ushers will see to it that the area is cleared before the ceremony begins. As in home weddings, you can drape stanchions leading to the altar area, but a garland attached to the railing of the steps that lead from the house or porch will suffice.

Once again, anything that can be replanted is preferable to the "cut-and-died" varieties.

Bouquets for the Bride and Bridesmaids

Said Connie Plaissay of the Plaza Florist in New York, "The only time I refuse to do a wedding is when 'mother' starts taking over. Once I told one that I'd do her wedding first, then her daughter's. Another time, I made a deal with the bride: I gave her three years to pay for it all herself. Then *she* picked the flowers."

Even if your mother isn't insisting on stephanotis, wedding bouquets should reflect your personal choice, although you might need to do some solid research. With the help of a professional designer, the bridal magazines, and your own knowledge of flowers, you can take this alien object—the bouquet—and make it your own. The first thing you may want to know is whether a bouquet is even necessary. No, it is not. But, aside from being pretty and traditional, it does serve an important purpose—it gives your hands something to do besides fidget. Bridesmaids, too, walk more easily and gracefully with flowers in hand.

Bouquets vary in shape and styling and should suit your dress and the mood of your wedding. A good flower designer will want to know all the details before recommending a particular idea. If you're short and stocky, he'll suggest an arm bouquet rather than a round arrangement. As one pro explained, "If someone hands you a booklet and says, 'Look through this, honey,' you should find another florist."

The basic shapes include traditional cascades, round nosegays, long-stemmed arm arrangements, hearth baskets, single flowers, or sprays. You can also carry a prayer book with flowers attached. Traditional bouquets are composed of three elements: (1) the flowers themselves; (2) fillers, such as baby's breath, Queen Anne's lace, or candytuft; and (3) greens, such as ivy, lemon leaves, or ferns. Aside from the labor involved, the cost of your bouquet will be determined by the number and type of real flowers used, and it is a good idea to know the ratio of flowers to filler to leaves before the wedding day.

You can mix different varieties for a field flower effect, but it's best to select small-headed types such as freesias, delphiniums, tea roses, or cymbidium orchids rather than their full-blown relatives, for one large flower like a chrysanthemum or peony will overpower the rest. Also, formal flowers such as mums, calla lilies, rubrum lilies, long-stemmed roses, peonies, and irises give wonderful solo performances, and they should never be relegated to a choir or otherwise cut down to size.

If the traditional choices don't appeal to you, there are alternatives. A small lace shoulder pouch could be stuffed with a tiny posy; gold rope or braiding could be laced with flowers and worn as a belt or draped from shoulder to hip. Don't get too contrived, though, and decide to fill a knapsack with stalks of lilac or forsythia. Silk or dried flowers can also be used, and these will, of course, be a permanent memento of the wedding.

Tips about Bouquets

1. Ask your florist to wire and wrap the flowers for your bouquet. Otherwise, he'll use plastic holders filled with oasis or styrofoam, which are awkward, heavy, and have been known to drip.

2. Say no to the paper doily that is supposed to look like real lace. If you have your own crocheted lace doily, have him use it.

3. Want a bow and streamers? Provide him with good double-faced satin ribbon, or tie it yourself.

4. You can dry some or all of your bouquet flowers by tying them together and hanging them upside down in a dark, dry area for about two weeks.

5. Make your own potpourri by crushing the dried flowers, adding spices, attar, and orange or lemon peel. Wrap the mixture in a lace handkerchief.

6. You can save money if you make your own bouquet, but without some expertise, don't attempt anything more ambitious than an informal arrangement of loosely tied long-stemmed flowers.

Boutonnieres and Corsages

There are two important things you need to know about boutonnieres: the groom wears a special one, and they are always pinned to the left lapel. Corsages for mothers and grandmothers are traditional, but shouldn't conflict with their dresses. They can be worn at the wrist, pinned to a dress or jacket, or tied to a handbag or even to grandmother's cane.

Wedding Transportation

I saw a beautiful sight not long ago in a sleepy New England fishing village. A procession of dressed-up people, led by the bride and groom, were walking from the church to the American Legion building where a reception was to be held. I stopped one of the guests to ask what was going on, and he explained that the invitation said,

"Weather permitting, we invite you to walk with us to the reception." It was marvelous. Shopkeepers came out to cheer the group on, passersby clapped at the sight, and one little boy stopped to salute what he thought was a Veteran's Day parade! Chances are, a new tradition was started in that little town.

A month later, I caught up with the bride and asked her about the pageant. She was embarrassed at the thought that it may have been too showy. "But," she explained, "driving a car for a quarter of a mile is even more pretentious. In this town, walking distance starts at a mile."

You can get to and from the church on time in anything from a bicycle built for two to a traditional limousine. One couple sped off to their reception on a Harley-Davidson. Another took their time in a horse-drawn carriage. Still, most choose the convenience and economy of private cars.

In big cities, limousines are often provided for the wedding party. It's not that city slickers are accustomed to the luxury, but finding a parking space is usually impossible. One New York couple came up with a down-to-earth approach. They hired Checker taxicabs to take them to the church and later to the club. The cabbie in the lead car tied paper wedding bells to the change cup and replaced his dashboard statue with a wedding cake bride and groom. For guests, a double-decker city bus was hired to provide transportation to the reception. The fee was about the same as the cost of limousines.

Parking

It may be necessary to notify your local police department about the wedding so that they can assign a traffic officer. At the reception site, valet parking might be what you need. In big cities, you might want to recommend a parking garage to guests who will be driving in from out of town. If possible, reserve some space at that garage so they're not greeted with, "Sorry, full." If everyone will be gathering at a house or garden where parking is allowed on only one side of the street, the police can waive that restriction if you notify them in advance.

Gratuities

Flat rates for limousines usually include driver tips. If not, up to 15 percent is customary.

Long-distance Transportation for Guests

Even though you're not supposed to pay lodging or transportation costs for guests, you should help them with reservations and logistics as much as possible. When my friends Esther and Stan were married, they extended themselves in every way possible for the many out-of-town friends and relatives who wouldn't miss it for the world. The wedding was to take place near Detroit at her brother's house on Sunday, and people were to arrive the day before. As soon as the RSVPs were in, Esther sent the following letter:

> Needless to say, Stan and I are deeply touched and pleased that you will be traveling to Michigan for our wedding. As you know, Detroit and New York have shared equally as homes dear to my heart, and your presence at our marriage makes it possible for us to share this joyous moment with friends and family all together. How ever lucky we both feel . . . thank you.
>
> Now, how to make the trek as painless as possible!
>
> We've assumed that most of the out-of-town guests would be arriving in the Detroit area on Saturday afternoon and want to depart after the wedding on Sunday evening. My dear cousins, Beatrice and Ben, have also assumed this, since they are planning a Saturday-night dinner party at their home in Farmington at 7 P.M. to which you and all the guests coming in from out of town are cordially invited.
>
> To help with your travel planning, Lynn at LINDEN TRAVEL (41 East 57 St., N.Y. Telephone 212 421-3320) is on the alert and will be pleased to handle ticketing and hotels. We are suggesting the following:
>
> For guests traveling by air:

*Sat. 8/18, Amer. Airlines #481	Depart LaGuardia	1:30 P.M.
	Arrive Detroit	3:09 P.M.
*Sun. 8/19, Amer. Airlines #586	Depart Detroit	7:00 P.M.
	Arrive LaGuardia	8:26 P.M.

*A group fare has been arranged and can be ticketed directly from Linden Travel

Sat. 8/18, Amer. Airlines #68	Depart Los Angeles	9:00 A.M.
	Arrive Detroit	4:05 P.M.

Sun. 8/19, United Airlines #85	Depart Detroit	9:00 P.M.
	Arrive Los Angeles	10:30 P.M.

We will be arranging transportation to and from the Detroit airport, and will give you details on this later.

From other cities:

If you are arriving on Saturday, it would be helpful if you could time your arrival to the Detroit airport around 3 or 4 P.M. But not to worry if this isn't possible. Please let us know your specific arrival information; we will make plans to meet you accordingly.

Hotel:

We are recommending the SOMERSET INN, 2601 West Big Beaver Rd., Troy, Michigan 48084, (313) 643-7800, which is about 40 minutes from the Detroit Metro Airport, and about 15 minutes from the festivities.

Forgive the formality of this form letter. I felt you would all understand how much easier it would be for me if I could put this all down in writing once—for all.

God bless and love,

Later, each guest received a personal itinerary confirming all arrangements, including minibus transportation and a timetable of social events. Stan and Esther couldn't have made it easier for their guests and harder for themselves. But there were no regrets, since everything went smoothly.

You certainly don't have to be as ambitious or extravagant, but try to get Uncle Jack or some of the ushers or bridesmaids to shuttle carless guests and make them feel at home in your town.

Recording the Ceremony

Even technophobes want pictures or tapes of their weddings. Most will settle for a leather-bound album filled with formal and candid prints of the ceremony and reception. Others will brave the world of electronics and have a videotape or disc made that can be played back through a television system. You can slip a microcassette recorder into an usher's pocket, ask your nephew who fancies himself the next John Ford to shoot some Super-8 film, or accept your friend's offer to shoot some 35-mm slides. But if you really want a permanent record of your wedding, leave it up to the pros.

I've heard story after story of amateur failures. You know, that new high-speed film really needed a flash after all. Or, even though they're black and white, we could tint the prints in sepia. Or, I didn't know *that* was your mother!

As always, your clergyman will have to approve any filming that will take place in the church or synagogue. And you should find out how disruptive it may be to have cables and lights set up. Flashes can mar the dignity of a ceremony. Ask the photographer to shoot high-speed film in available light. Flashes are not as intrusive during the recessional.

Aside from the wedding album itself, there are two things that will give you a great deal of pleasure. If you don't own the equipment, borrow, rent, or buy it for future use. One is a microcassette tape recorder, about the size of a cigarette pack. The tiny tapes run up to 60 minutes and will record well from about 10 feet if there is no interference. Anyone, even the groom, the clergyman, or the bride herself can carry it to the altar, or hide it ABSCAM style in a pocket or purse. These recorders start at about $50 and go up. I like Sony's model, which is more expensive. Test the machine before you use it, of course.

The other item is Polaroid's new SX-70 Sonar Instant-picture camera. There's nothing like leaving the party with a fistful of photos to enjoy on your honeymoon. The camera costs around $200; the film is about $8 per 10 shots; and the flashbars are about $3 for 10 flashes. Ask a friend or relative to do the honors. They need only compose the picture; the rest is done automatically.

12 • The Reception

The horror stories abound: The reception that was delayed by an hour and a half because of a photo session that should have taken no more than 15 minutes. The caterer who had the gall to ring a dinner bell to get everyone seated. The bandleader who fancied himself the Bert Parks of wedding receptions, manipulating the crowd with every tiresome wedding cliché he could think of. As one bride put it, "It's like hiring a decorator—you have to approve the selections every step of the way. For the first time in my life, I got to be really bossy."

You don't have to spend six months in an assertiveness training program to have a great wedding reception, but you do have to pin down an agenda and set the style, starting with any customary wedding rituals you may want.

Traditions

The Receiving Line

Except when a church wedding is followed by a smaller, private reception, the receiving line is usually formed at the reception after the formal photographs are taken. The purpose is to give the bride and groom, the hosts, and the honored members of the wedding party a chance to greet the guests formally and accept their good wishes. If the reception is for fifty people or less, a receiving line is unnecessary. For seventy-five people, it's optional. But if you're having a big crowd, you'll never get to see everyone without it.

Here's how the receiving line works. The hosts, often the parents of the bride, are first; then come the groom's parents, the bride and groom, the maid and matron of honor, and the bridesmaids. The fathers and bridesmaids also have the option, instead, of circulating among the guests and making them feel welcome. The ushers and best man do not traditionally participate, but you can certainly create a receiving line that includes them or any other people who may belong there.

For example, if a friend or friends have agreed to host the reception, they should stand in the line to greet strangers who have come to their home. A favorite grandmother or aunt can be asked to join, but may certainly decline if it represents too much of a physical strain. If your kid brother is an usher and you want him to stand with you, that's okay, too. Divorced parents can stand together or be separated by the groom's parents.

Flower girls and ring bearers are not included—for their sakes. If you were a five-year-old, would you want to get pinched on the cheek one hundred times? Besides, little kids have too much energy to stand still for any great length of time, and they shouldn't be expected to.

At very large formal weddings, an announcer introduces guests to the bride's mother as they pass through the line. If your mother doesn't know a lot of the guests, the announcer can be helpful, but his real function is to keep that line moving quickly so as not to delay the start of the reception.

Your parents' job is to make people feel welcome. From "How good of you to come such a long distance," to "I've been looking forward to meeting you," to "Jim has spoken so highly of you," parents are supposed to keep smiling and offering a generous dose of hospitality.

The bride should personalize her welcome, if possible. For example, "We love the silver service, and we can't wait to use it," or "I hope you didn't have any trouble driving in from Smithtown with all that construction." The bride also introduces family members or friends to her husband, if he doesn't know them, and vice versa.

The groom will have the toughest time. He'll have to field "congratulations," or "what a handsome couple," or, in some cases, some truly tasteless remarks. He usually shakes hands and thanks people for their good wishes.

The guests should introduce themselves, if there is no announcer, and "be happy to meet" the lineup. The bride and groom get best wishes or congratulations, and kisses are allowed to those you know well. (The old tradition that the bride should never be congratulated is over.) Above all, keep the line moving, and don't discuss the latest economic trends or have lengthy conversations.

You can ask people to sign a guest book, but with all the assembling for the receiving line, it could clog the works. If guests are to be given seat assignments for a sit-down dinner, however, they may get their table numbers while signing the register.

Seating Arrangements

There can be a "bridal table" where the couple, their attendants, and their attendants' spouses or dates sit facing the room, but you can decide to be a lot more casual than that, integrating members of the wedding party with other guests, perhaps flanking yourselves with your maid of honor and her spouse and the best man and his wife or girl friend. In either case, the bride and groom should circulate from table to table and say hello, again, to everyone.

It is customary to seat all the parents together and a few select people from each family to fill out that honorary table. The clergyman or officiant and his wife (her husband) are also seated at the parents' table.

Seating the guests is perhaps the greatest test of a good hostess. If you get it right, your guests will have a wonderful time. If you don't, they may leave before you do. In a recent issue of *Cosmopolitan,* Michaele Weissman writes about "Surviving Other People's Weddings." She says, "This issue of where you sit is serious. At the wedding of my cousin Nat, I was actually seated at the teen table. The way Aunt Ruth sees it, if you're not married, you are not grown-up. I don't know when *you* last had a fifteen-year-old for a dinner partner, but let me tell you, trying to talk to one is about as rewarding as bailing out the *Bismarck* with an ice bucket."

Single people should not be ostracized from the "legitimate couples" any more than that old tradition of separating husbands and wives should be enforced. There are, of course, some special interest groups which deserve their own place at your wedding, especially little kids and teen-agers. They'd rather be among themselves than on their best behavior with a group of scrutinizing adults.

Toasts

After guests pass through the receiving line, champagne is served to a standing crowd; or, if formal seating is arranged, the champagne is poured at the tables. Traditionally, the first toast is proposed by the best man. Then the groom, ushers, and fathers may offer their own words. But where is it written that the women can't make toasts and be as witty and wise—or even sentimental—as the men?

More and more, matrons and maids of honor, as well as brides themselves, have a few words to say to their hosts or parents, their attendants, and their spouses. No matter who speaks, it makes sense to put someone in charge (perhaps an honor attendant) of organizing the speakers in some kind of order and with a timetable.

The best toasts are both funny and loving, and always gracious. Without turning the toast into a roast, the best man, usually a longtime friend of the groom, might comment tastefully on his friend's errant youth. If friends or relatives are hosting the reception, the bride and groom or the parents should acknowledge their generosity through a special toast.

Don't forget that little tape recorder. This is a good time to use the flip side.

The First Dance

With or without some signal from the bandleader, the bride's first dance is always with her husband, but there are two ways to proceed after that dance is well under way. Customarily, the bride's father will ask the groom's mother to dance, and the groom's father will ask the bride's mother at the same time. Then the attendants can join in, followed by the guests. The alternative is for the bride's father to cut in on the groom and for the groom to dance with the bride's mother; the groom's father then cuts in, dancing with the bride while the bride's father dances with his new in-law. Attendants can then join in, followed by the guests.

However you choose to kick up your heels, make sure everyone knows what to do and when to do it. Don't let the bandleader take over by calling out names and instructions.

Cutting the Cake

It is part of a traditional reception for the bride and groom to cut and eat the first slice of wedding cake. But they needn't stuff it in each other's mouths as if they were in a pablum feeding contest. If you want to eat your cake publicly, make sure a small plate and one or two forks are provided.

Bouquets and Garters

You don't have to throw your bouquet, a garter, or anything else, but if you want to, gather the bridesmaids or other unmarried women around and pitch the bouquet up so it will fall lightly to the crowd. If you aim it like a forward pass, you'll risk fumbles or even injuries. Garters are thrown to the ushers. The groom removes it, and you toss it.

Unwanted Rituals

All of a sudden, some not too sober relative might pick up his spoon and start clinking his wineglass. Others follow. Soon the whole room sounds like a herd of bulls in a china shop. What to do? Kiss him, no matter how much you hate the idea of bussing on demand. It's the only way to prevent all the crystal from being demolished.

Guests can get carried away, especially if they've had a lot to drink. One bride remembered a nightmarish moment: "I was being carried off in a chair by some drunken friends toward the dance floor. I thought they'd surely drop me or rip my veil. I was terrified."

You can't control everything that happens at your reception, and if you try to police behavior, you'll have a terrible time yourself. Plan what you can, and then let it happen.

Lighting and Color

No matter how large or small, plain or ornate your reception room may be, the color scheme and lighting are as important in setting the mood as the food and flowers are to a good party. Daytime weddings in rooms blessed with natural light are lovely, although bad weather might force the management to throw the switch. If soft incandescent light results, no problem; but in church halls and some clubrooms, overhead fluorescent bulbs are used, and nothing is less flattering than that. Find out if you can rent some lamps instead, and load each table with at least three votive candles as well, perhaps integrated into the floral centerpiece. Otherwise, hurricane lamps can be strategically placed to supplement the lighting you provide.

Evening receptions in rooms or halls should be planned the same way. Be sure to review the lighting system with the proprietor so you know what you're getting.

Daytime garden weddings are nature's way of helping you cope with the energy crisis, but if you like the idea of a reception under the stars on a balmy summer evening, be prepared to become a lighting engineer. First of all, torches, candleposts, or sand-filled cutout paper bags that hold votive candles should light the footpath from the street to the garden. The house itself probably has lights at the doorways and porches and may not need to be supplemented. Floodlights should be added to trees or spotted from windows to light dim corners, and oriental lanterns could be strung from trees to cordon off such areas as cutting gardens or pools. Little white Christmas lights—the ones that don't blink—can dress a tree or some shrubbery. The tent stakes, which can be hazardous in the dark, should be lighted by candles or spotted to avoid injury. But your greatest challenge and achievement will be the tent itself. Avoid bare light bulbs by covering them with rice-paper globes. For a festive effect, the center post can be braided and wrapped with greens and those little white Christmas lights. And the tables can be set with hurricane lamps or wick lanterns, both of which are impervious to the wind.

Color schemes usually start with the bridesmaids' dresses and the bouquets themselves and remain consistent with the floral arrangements, tablecloths, napkins, and other room decorations. The most desirable tones are peach and pink because any reflections of these colors from clothes or room accessories flatter the complexion. Blues, lavenders, and greens are also attractive, and because they are cool colors, they are often used for summer weddings. Yellow and orange are fine for accents, but a solid dose sallows the complexion and gives everything a slightly jaundiced look. Pure white tablecloths are fine, and they look festive with multicolored floral arrangements.

Bold primaries can be dynamic in the right setting, with bouquets of tulips or anemones to bring the joyful colors home, but they shouldn't fight with their surroundings. If the room is pastel and subtle, you can brighten it, but don't overwhelm it with purple, red, and yellow.

The Food

For a small home or garden wedding, you can do your own cooking and hire people to serve and clean up. You can even ask friends to bring a covered dish for your small, intimate reception. If you're planning a wedding that's grand or formal, however, you'll probably rely on the catering services of a club, hotel, or restaurant or choose an independent to do the job at home.

Most caterers provide everything you'll need for the perfect party: food, staff (waiters, bartenders in uniform), tables, chairs, barware, plates, flatware, linens, liquor, cake—even music and flowers. Some itemize these costs; others have an all-inclusive per-head price, which varies according to menu selections and other options. There are, however, average costs for catered receptions. The following breakdown is based on a sampling of big-city catering establishments that offer gourmet selections. They are not from the onion-dip school of hors d'oeuvres and their prices reflect that.

The Cocktail Reception:
$25 per person (2 hours)

Food (hot and cold hors d'oeuvres)	$10.00
Liquor (cocktails, 1 round champagne)	7.50
Staff (1 bartender, 2 waitresses)	4.00
Rentals (glasses, napkins, chairs, bar table, cloth)	3.50

Total: $25.00 per person
(add $2.00 if caterer provides cake)

The Buffet Breakfast or Brunch:
$30–$35 per person (3 hours)

Food (hot and cold menu, no hors d'oeuvres)	$15.00
Liquor (champagne, bloody marys, wine)	7.50

Staff	5.00
Rentals (tables, chairs, linens, plates, flatware, barware, etc.)	6.00
	Total: $33.50 per person

The Buffet Luncheon or Dinner, Plus Cocktails: $40–$55 per person (4 hours)

Hors d'oeuvres	$ 8.00
Food	15.00
Liquor (cocktails, wine, 1 round champagne)	10.00
Staff	8.00
Rentals	6.00
	Total: $47.00 per person

The Sit-Down Luncheon or Dinner, Plus Cocktails: $60–$100 per person (5 hours)

Hors d'oeuvres	$10.00
Food	20.00
Liquor (cocktails, wine, champagne, brandy)	15.00
Staff	16.00
Rentals	10.00
	Total: $71.00 per person

Taxes and Tips

When you hire a caterer, you'll probably be asked to sign a contract and leave a deposit (anywhere from 10 to 50 percent of the total estimated cost). The state tax varies according to where you live, but it should also be estimated on that contract. Some establishments—especially hotels, catering halls, restaurants, and clubs—will automatically add a percentage for gratuities, but the independent caterers usually rely on your generosity in this regard. You don't tip the owner, but you do provide for his staff. The supervisor who oversees the staff gets anywhere from $15 to $25; the chef, $15 to $20; bartenders, $10 to $15; and waitresses and busboys, $5 to $10. For cloakroom and powder-room attendants, arrange a flat fee with the management, and make sure a sign is posted in both areas indicating that gratuities have been provided by the host.

Finding the Ideal Caterer

Most people find their caterers through other people. The personal recommendation is so successful that one New York catering company calls itself Word of Mouth. If this doesn't work for you, try to remember the business parties you've attended recently that impressed you most. Call the public relations office of the firm that hosted the event and get the name of the caterer. Or check the society column in your local newspaper. If a party sounds particularly appealing, call the editor and try to find out who did the catering.

Once you've settled on one or more candidates, compare prices and menus. Don't hesitate to ask how many twenty-inch trays of marinated shrimp are included in the cocktail fare, or how many cold canapés are placed in the brioche shell. If smoked salmon is offered, is it a full side, or less? If the caterer says, "Madam, please leave it up to us," explain that you prefer to know exactly what you are paying for. If he or she still doesn't cooperate, take your business elsewhere. Some caterers will let you sample the selections for free; others will charge a fee. Banquet managers can usually arrange for you and your fiancé to sample the meal they'll serve, and you can also pay to taste the wines and champagne. Once you've decided whom to hire and worked out the timing, the menu, and the decorations, let the caterer do the job without undue interference.

Entertaining Large Groups

In the last 10 years, Americans have had a love affair with food that has turned even die-hard meat and potato men into experts on nouvelle cuisine. Still, no matter how sophisticated we've become, you can't expect a large and divergent group to all enjoy some exotic Mongolian dish. Happily, there is a wide-ranging medium between surf and turf and the adventurous world of Turkish peasant food. Your caterer will, no doubt, suggest a variety of main courses or buffet items within your budget. Here are some do's and don'ts for a successful menu prepared either by a caterer or yourself.

General. Don't use paper plates, napkins, plastic glasses, or plastic knives and forks; rent or borrow what you need. Ethnic food is fine, but when you serve it, also serve something traditional for those whose tastes are not so venturesome.

For cocktail parties. Avoid messy foods, such as quiches, that need a plate and fork; people can't hold a drink and eat comfortably. One-bite finger food is preferable. When any tray of hors d'oeuvres is being passed, make sure the waiter identifies it to the guests; a statement such as, "Would you care for some clam fingers?" might spare a friend who's allergic to shellfish from a disastrous reaction. Balance the selections among fish, meat, vegetables, breads, and cheeses.

For buffets. Set up the table of food to allow an easy flow of traffic. Nothing is worse than waiting interminably on a food line. If people will be balancing plates on their laps rather than sitting at tables, be sure the food is easy to cut and manage. Ragoûts or very tender slices of roast meats are preferable to steaks, chops, or other hard-to-cut entrées. Offer at least one vegetarian dish, such as a rice salad with blanched vegetables. For a large, formal buffet, have at least two people serving from each end of the table.

For sit-down meals. Chicken, beef, and veal are across-the-board favorites for main courses. Balance each course; don't serve cream of asparagus soup followed by chicken breasts in cream sauce. Most people agree that if salads are to be served at all, they should follow the meal; the reason is that the vinegar in the dressing fights with the subtle taste of the wine. Don't expect your caterer to successfully serve a pasta course to two hundred people. Since pasta must be cooked at the last minute for a particularly short period of time, it would be difficult, if not impossible, to prepare and serve it perfectly for more than fifty people.

Catering Your Own Reception

Unless your kitchen is large and stocked with professional equipment, you shouldn't consider preparing a reception for more than fifty people. If you are going to do it, here's a step-by-step planning guide:

1. Plan a menu for which everything can be bought, prepared, and stored in advance.

2. Make arrangements to rent or borrow the glasses, flatware, plates, linens, chairs, etc., from a party rental service. If you expect to give one or more parties a year, you might consider buying your plates and flatware from a restaurant supply shop. These are easy to store. Barware is usually too bulky for easy storage and should be rented.

3. Make arrangements through a catering, bartending, or party service to hire a bartender and at least one waiter who will also clean up. Their fees range from ten to fifteen dollars per hour, often with a 4-hour minimum, not including tip. Have them arrive half an hour before the guests so they can change and be given instructions.

4. The waiter or bartender can arrange to bring the ice. Otherwise, order it from an independent service.

5. Order wines, liquors, and mixers, and arrange for delivery well in advance of the wedding.

6. Order the cake from a local baker, or accept the offer of a friend to bake it for you. If you want to make it and decorate it yourself, arrange to refrigerate it at a friend's or neighbor's house.

7. Ask at least one friend, relative, or your groom to be there to help you with the cooking, organizing, and preparation.

8. Set up the food table (but not the food) at least 6 hours before the wedding. Have serving pieces identified for the staff. You may set up the bar yourself, although some bartenders prefer to do it themselves. Check first.

9. Rely on the Yellow Pages if friends can't recommend these services.

All of the following meals were prepared by brides without the help of a professional caterer. In the case of the hot luncheon, the kitchen was already equipped with double ovens to accommodate heating the trays of chicken. Note that both hot food menus featured rice rather than potatoes or pasta. With one exception, premixed packages were used. Two of the brides offered an alternative to the wedding cake. One served sherbet, the other a selection of fruits.

The Buffet Brunch

I. Cheese and spinach quiches
Mixed green salad with vinaigrette
Prosciutto or sliced Westphalian ham and melon
Cheeses (Brie or triple crème, chèvre, Edam, or Gouda)
Sliced smoked salmon, garnished with capers and onions
Croissants or baguettes of French bread
Selection of jams, marmalade

II. Chicken, crab meat, and spinach crepes, heated and served with a cream sauce
Mixed green salad with vinaigrette dressing
Pâté
French bread

The Cold Buffet Luncheon

Fish mousse
Pasta or rice salad
Salade nicoise or mixed shellfish salad with a creamy dill dressing or vinaigrette
Chicken salad with capers
Selection of breads

The Hot Buffet Luncheon

I. Suprêmes de volaille
Asparagus in butter sauce
White and wild rice
Sliced tomatoes with watercress
Bread

II. Chicken tarragon
Mixed green salad with sliced fresh mushrooms
Glazed carrots
Rice pilaf
Bread

The Cocktail Reception

Crab claws with cocktail sauce or mayonnaise curry dip
Filo triangles, stuffed with spinach, cheese, and meat (made and frozen one month before)

Crudités with anchovy dip
Baked new potatoes, halved, topped with sour cream and caviar
Sliced pâté
Full wheel of Brie with French bread
Humus with pita bread

Cocktails and Dinner Buffet

I. Mixed nuts
Cold shrimp with cocktail sauce
Cherry tomatoes stuffed with Boursin cheese

Ragoût of lamb in dill and sour cream sauce
Rice pilaf
Endive and watercress salad

II. Smoked oysters with rice crackers
Fried zucchini sticks garnished with lemon
Swedish meatballs

Blanquette de veau
White and wild rice
Green beans with sliced almonds
Bread

Unusual Receptions

There are, of course, hundreds of different ways to plan a wedding reception. None of them is necessarily the right way or the only way to do it, but you should be sensitive to the needs and wants of your guests. Would your relatives really enjoy a no-holds-barred reception at the local disco, with lights flashing, music blasting, and bodies thrashing? Probably not. But they might love an old-fashioned barbecue followed by a barn dance. One couple did it at her father's ranch. Legend goes that the party went on for three days. The barbecue was something else. Ribs, chicken, teriyaki shrimp, corn on the cob, huge vats of potato salad, hamburgers and hot dogs for the kids, sour mash punch, and a homemade supply of corn whiskey. Add a cake topped with a bride and groom on horseback, the best country music in the area, and you've got a great party.

On a Cape Cod beach, about 50 yards from the house, the greatest clambake in the history of New England was held. It just happened to be a wedding reception. There were lobsters galore, with barrels of clams and mussels. Plus chicken, salad, and all you could drink. Swimming was definitely permitted. The music was simple: one guitar and a whole lot of people singing every old song they could remember.

Here's a new one: the elegantly catered picnic reception. Each guest was provided with a box luncheon, a choice of red or white wine, and tables or blankets. It was all arranged with permission from a state park. The music was a string quartet that really gave a concert on the lawn.

Drinks

Most hotels, restaurants, or clubs don't allow you to supply your own liquor or wine. If they do, there will be a corkage fee (and it could be exorbitant), so you may or may not save money. If you can bring some of your own liquor, make sure you buy the champagne.

Because champagne is so expensive, it is worth discussing the various kinds available and the alternatives. Champagne is really sparkling wine made in the region of Champagne in France. And even though producers outside of that area may have the same high production standards (fermenting the wine in the bottle in which it is sold), they may not, according to French law, call it champagne. France in particular produces a lot of sparkling wines, as do Germany, Italy, and Spain. But the United States is catching up. We may call it champagne, but we identify it as either California or New York State.

Wine expert Frank Prial explains that a good champagne or sparkling white wine requires expert handling. He says that some companies use the vat process of production, which is inferior to even the transfer method, where the wine is fermented in one bottle and then removed to another, leaving the sediment behind. His advice: if you can't afford the real stuff at $20 to $40 a bottle, you can do very well for $8 to $12 in sparkling wine that's labeled *"méthode champenoise."* Buy one or two different brands before the wedding and try it out together. If you don't think you can kill two bottles or more and still make it to the office the next day, ask a few close friends over for dinner and get their opinions. The average bottle of champagne (26 ounces) yields 8 servings. Therefore, for a hundred guests to have one drink each, you'd need a case (12 bottles).

At the reception, after the first round is served for the toasts, you needn't offer more, but if you want it available to those people who really appreciate the bubbly, have at least one more case on hand. Remember that champagne needs to be chilled before serving. Filling washtubs with ice and carefully nestled champagne bottles is the best way to keep it cold.

For very simple receptions, it is okay to serve a champagne punch, but many people don't like it, especially if it's their only choice.

If you're having an elegant sit-down dinner, it is generous but not necessary to place a bottle of brandy on each table after the cake has been served. Otherwise, waiters may offer sweet liqueurs or brandies from a cart, or take orders.

You don't have to offer pink ladies and piña coladas to make your guests happy, but in addition to the standard mixers (club soda, seltzer, ginger ale, tonic water, bitter lemon), you should have lime, orange, and lemon juice on hand for daiquiris, mimosas, sours, and screwdrivers. Cassis makes a wine cocktail called Kir. For morning or early-afternoon weddings, tomato juice and spices should be available for bloody marys.

Stocking the Bar

The trick is to know a little bit about the drinking habits of your family and friends. There's no doubt that, during the last few years, Americans have shifted their allegiance from martinis to white wine. And vodka is challenging scotch as a national favorite. According to one major liquor distributor, white liquors such as vodka, gin, and light rum are outselling the traditional scotch, bourbon, and blended whiskeys respectively.

The national trends do not, however, account for regional preferences. If you live in the South, fine bourbon is a must. In the North, scotch is more popular. And in California, where the white wine craze was born, there's talk that "hot tub" gin is gaining.

Whether it's because of the Perrier campaign or the latest fad diet, sparkling waters have become as popular at the bar as Coke is at the soda fountain.

In summer months, vodka and gin (mixed with tonic or soda) will be more popular. In cold weather, the darker, richer whiskeys will move. Calculate all the information you have, and figure on the following: if your bartender averages a drink at 1½ ounces, a quart of liquor will yield twenty drinks. You can estimate that the average person will consume 4 to 5 drinks in the course of an evening. This is true for Perrier people, too. Guests who drink wine exclusively will each consume a bottle or more. The following chart gives a hypothetical profile of one hundred wedding guests.

Number of guests (based on 100)	Item	Measurement	Amount to Buy
20	Vodka	5 drinks each	5 quarts
15	Scotch	5 drinks each	4 quarts
10	Gin	5 drinks each	3 fifths
10	Bourbon	5 drinks each	3 fifths
10	Other	5 drinks each	
	Light rum		
	Blended whiskey		
	Vermouth, sweet and dry		1 fifth each
	Sherry, sweet and dry		
25	Wine	1 bottle each	2 cases white
			1 case red
10	water, soda, beer	totally generous to account for mixed liquor drinks as well	1 case club soda
			1 case seltzer
			1 case tonic
			1 case ginger ale
			1 mixed case Tab/cola
			1 case beer

It's perfectly possible that your guests will be 35 percent wine, 25 percent water and soda. If so, recalculate the chart, limiting the hard liquor accordingly. Also, if you're serving wine with a meal, you'll probably have to double the order.

Money saver. Most establishments will charge you only for the bottles opened, and they will see to it that there's enough of everything to provide an open bar. But if you're buying the booze yourself, ask if the liquor store will allow you to return unopened bottles. Most will, knowing full well that you'll shop around until you find some cooperation. This way, you won't get caught short.

Unfortunate Situations

Some people simply have never learned how to drink well. Others set out to get drunk. Still others are victims of alcoholism. Without hiring a representative from AA to troubleshoot your wedding, you should be aware of the following information. Salty foods make people drink more (this is a good excuse to skip the caviar). High-protein foods help replenish the supply of blood sugar lost by drinking alcohol (heavy on the Swedish meatballs). Coffee doesn't help—all it does is make a slightly sleepy drunk more awake. But water, lots of it, with aspirin, will bring someone back to his or her senses.

I was at one wedding recently where a dozen or more so-called friends were freely passing marijuana and snorting cocaine. Even though some couples have received and presumably enjoyed wedding gifts of cocaine and marijuana, it seems particularly rude to play your own private movies at someone else's wedding. Any argument that suggests that using drugs is like drinking alcohol is nonsense. Moderate drinking is an acceptable social activity. Drugs, in my experience, bring on a dreamy narcissism that preempts human contact instead of encouraging it. Most guests will refrain from using drugs at a wedding, respecting the occasion and the families involved. But it doesn't hurt to pass the word to your friends as a precaution.

The Music

Some weddings don't make it because someone else is always in charge, such as a caterer or a social director. The bride, groom, and guests are simply swept away in a sea of programmed fun that minimizes their own responsibility and maximizes the power of the hired help. It was in this setting that the master-of-ceremonies bandleader was born.

Many people who were not used to entertaining large groups encouraged the bandleader to take control of the party. The result was a "wedding act" that was developed by bands to satisfy the lack of individual flair that marks many receptions. The introduction of the bride and groom to a drum roll; the who-dances-with-whom musical instruction speech; the silly "Bride Cuts the Cake" version of the "Farmer in the Dell"—all of these manipulative musical gestures are part of the act.

If you're not careful, you could be as embarrassed as the couple whose bandleader bellowed for guests to line up for the bunny hop. How can you avoid this? First, find out exactly how the band operates. If you must, crash another wedding to hear how they sound and see what they do. But you may not have to go to that extreme, since many bands let you audition them. Have a list of do's and don'ts, and discuss all the arrangements with the bandleader. Tell him (or her) what kind of music you'd like to hear; give him some specific selections to play; find out how long the breaks are, etc. Most bands will do whatever you want without feeling threatened or insulted.

A band is probably the most expensive music you can provide for your wedding. Costs vary greatly, spiraling upward if a prominent bandleader such as Lester Lanin comes personally instead of sending his second string. Also, union wages are usually higher than nonunion and can affect the final cost.

If you don't want a full-scale band, but still want to dance, a three- or four-piece combo will do. Two guitars and a drum; a guitar, piano, and drum; or a guitar, electric organ, and drum. Any of these instruments will give a big sound when electrically amplified.

Harpsichords, violins, cellos, harps, violas—these strings can create beautiful music, but don't expect people to kick up their heels dancing. This sound is nearly always sedate rather than rousing, and therefore perfect for cocktail receptions, where people can easily talk above the music.

A solo pianist, harpist, violinist, or classical guitarist can add the perfect musical touch to a small reception where the acoustics are no problem.

Another idea is to contact a local school of music or conservatory where musical talent abounds at nonprofessional prices. Most schools, such as the famed Juilliard School of Music in New York, post these requests on a "job offering" bulletin board. You can usually audition the talent and hire them at a lower fee.

You can rent a disco sound system—with a disc jockey—that is similar to what is used in discotheques, but portable. You can work with the disc jockey on selections. Most have a repertoire that goes beyond new wave rock, but you may have to provide some of the records or tapes yourself. The cost is about $400 for the average wedding, depending on travel expenses.

A tape cassette system can give you ninety minutes of uninterrupted music. You can make the tape yourself, varying the selections to include some disco, swing, classical, country, jazz, rock, or whatever you like. You can borrow most of the records you'll want in order to create the tape or tapes, and you will save a lot of money in the process. Remember that tapes exceeding ninety minutes are thin and therefore more vulnerable to distortion and breakage.

Flowers and Plants

Like bandleaders and caterers, florists have a Pavlovian reaction to weddings. So many of their creative ideas have been rejected by diehard traditionalists that they automatically think in terms of pink roses and baby's breath. Just mention the possibility of anemones or rubrum lilies, and their eyes will start to shine with a glimmer of hope that suggests, Maybe this wedding will be different.

Unless you want to go to the expense of having special flowers flown in from Europe, Hawaii, or other places, your selections will be limited by the season. Sit down with your florist and discuss your color theme, room(s), tables, cake, and any other areas of floral decoration. Go through the decorating and bridal magazines for ideas to see if it's possible to duplicate any arrangements for your reception. Bear in mind that flower costs have skyrocketed in the last few years, mostly because so many nurseries in the United States have gone out of business.

Table Centerpieces

If you can't afford cut flower arrangements for the tables and don't want to settle for daisies and carnations, there are other choices.

One designer I know calls it "greens n' weeds," and it is fabulous. He takes a selection of greenery—such as fragrant eucalyptus, lemon leaves, ferns, and ivy—adds delicate sprigs of baby's breath, Queen Anne's lace, or dried stalks of wheat, dune grass, or cattails, and *voilà:* the perfect centerpiece.

Another option is to use dried flowers, such as everlastings, wheat, statice, and baby's breath, which can be converted later by the florist into a large arrangement for your home.

Silk flowers, though expensive (anywhere from one to ten dollars for a single rose or peony), can be economical since they will last for years. These can also be mixed with greens, dried flowers, or even fresh flowers and collected later for conversion to a permanent table, floor, or wall arrangement.

I've been at elegant banquets where the table centerpieces were virtually edible. Fragrant fresh herbs, cut and mixed with candytuft, roses, or other flowers are attractive and inexpensive. Potted herbs mixed with sprigs of berries or flowers can be planted in the garden or kept alive on the windowsill. A florist may not stock herbs, but he can usually get them from a nursery or local greengrocer. You may save money by getting them yourself and having the caterer or florist design the arrangements.

Vegetable centerpieces are a creative way of serving the first course of crudités, and they can look fabulous. One caterer takes a head of leafy cabbage, hollows it out, and fills it with stalks of carrots, peeled and blanched asparagus, bleached mushrooms attached to a celery tree with toothpicks, radish rosettes, etc. The effect is stunning, inventive, and delicious when served with a light anchovy dip. Glazed or fresh fruits can also be used for centerpiece decoration, and subsequently, for dessert. Grapes and berries make good fillers.

A simple clay pot, or a series of pots in a basket, planted with begonias, impatiens, or miniature geraniums make lovely table arrangements that can be replanted as a wedding remembrance. In winter and early spring, pots of crocuses, dwarf tulips, hyacinths, and other bulb flowers are beautiful and will bloom perennially in a park or garden. Consult with your florist for a price on the plants themselves, the pots, and the baskets. Then compare these prices to those of a nursery. Make the best deal you can.

You can add charm to any flower arrangement with a creative touch of your own. One bride whose wedding had an oriental theme bought cheap wooden chopsticks, roped each pair in silver and gold string, bought gold paper fans, and had the florist stick them into a mossy basket filled with willow and quince blossoms.

If you like candles, long-burning votives are best, and your florist can incorporate them in any table arrangement. (Watch the time claims on the candles. Ones marked "12-hour" or "6-hour" rarely last anywhere near that long.) Tall tapers in holders, or hurricane lamps are fine for tables unaffected by air currents or crowding. If your reception is in a rented space, the management will control the candle placement. If you are at home, be smart and avoid even a minor fire by placing the candles carefully.

Flowers for the Reception Room

If the reception room is a big open space that needs a little help in the corners, rent trees from a nursery, a florist, or a plant shop. Potted palms or ficus, flowering azalea bushes, even hanging pots of simple grape ivy can mask a drab corner or the need for a new paint job.

For easy, graceful decoration, branches of dogwood, flowering quince, or other perennial trees and shrubs can be pretty and effective. If plants and flowers prove too costly or inadequate to reshape or camouflage a room, there is a time-consuming but inexpensive alternative—screens of sheeting. You take one-by-one-inch wood strips and nail them together to form each three-by-eight-foot panel frame. A minimum of three and a maximum of five panels make a good screen. Cut the sheeting (bought in a pattern that goes with your color scheme), and staple it at the back of each frame. Hinge the panels together and unfold the completed screen so that it is secure on the floor. Place a potted plant in front of it so that people won't lean against it or otherwise cause it to fall.

If your party is going to be held under a tent, you can cover the metal support posts with green leaves or a mixture of ribbon, greenery, baby's breath, or daisies. Bare light bulbs should also be shielded in some way without cutting the light source. Ground stakes can be lighted or tied with ribbons to avoid having someone trip on them.

Otherwise, tents take their decoration from the garden surroundings, the tables, the food, and the elegant array of guests.

Other Rooms

Flowers or scented candles should grace every room a guest may enter. Even the lowly toilet tank can be beautified by a nosegay of violets, although in this case the scented candle may be a better idea.

One bride filled a porcelain wall sconce with fresh flowers. She liked the effect so much that she replaced them later with permanent silk flowers.

For anterooms, vestibules, or other high traffic areas, fill a vase with long, lean flowers that can be set on a table or sill. Do not put anything breakable on the floor. You can fill an umbrella stand with branches of willow or quince, but don't place it in such a way that it cuts the flow of traffic.

Decorating the Cake with Flowers or Fruit

At one home wedding, a single-tier cake was designed by a French baker in conjunction with the florist. At the very center, a hole was cut, and a miniature vase was slipped into place and filled with tiny anemones. The cake was placed on a raised platter and the bottom level was strewn with the same anemones and baby's breath.

For tiered cakes, you can replace the plastic bridal couple with flowers in a similar way, or simply drape a braid of greenery and flowers onto the cake table's cloth.

Fruits, too, can be used for decoration. Sprigs of berries and grapes or glazed fruit sections can add a festive touch. Curled orange or lemon rinds twined with leaves are attractive and fragrant.

Recording the Reception

A successful art director decided to hire one of her favorite fashion photographers to shoot her wedding pictures. But the photographer, who was known for his stunning reportage approach to fashion, didn't quite measure up. Not only did he not get one complete shot of the entire wedding party, he also used 35-mm slides, resulting in poor prints of a series of arty candids.

This is not to say that artistic friends shouldn't photograph the wedding, too. But the best advice is to hire a professional wedding photographer to do the job right. Do, however, insist that he or she forget the contrived, predictable stuff—such as the two of you silhouetted against a stained-glass background. Your wedding, after all, shouldn't look like another Hallmark greeting card.

The formal shots of the wedding party are taken just before the reception begins. Typically, they include the following:

1. You and the groom
2. You with bridesmaids; him with groomsmen
3. You and him with the entire wedding party
4. You and him with each set of parents
5. Either or both of you with special members of the families

You can break down the list of formals any way you like, but the longer the list of "musts," the greater the delay of the reception.

Candid photos are a different story. They should record the day's events, starting with the hubbub in your house before the ceremony begins. For these pictures, your photographer will need some instruction. For example, "No, I don't want to be photographed with pink rollers in my hair." A good photographer will get the tears and laughs, the fooling around and the sober reflection without interrupting the mood or imposing himself too much.

And the reception is not a shoot-what-you-like affair. The photographer should snap all the special events, such as the dancing, the toasting, and the cake cutting. And special people should be pointed out: parents, grandmothers, and friends may not make the album without some prompting. In any case, before the wedding you and your pro will have a good idea of what's going to happen.

Bachrach Studios, a prominent portrait and wedding photography establishment, has a minimum order of $695. This includes a leather album with 40 color prints 8″ x 10″ a loose-leaf type album with the same 40 color prints 4″ x 5″; and one 11″ x 14″ color enlargement or six wallet-size reproductions of any one photograph. Prices vary, of course, but you should count on spending anywhere from $350 to $800 for your photos.

For an extra charge, you can usually order additional prints to frame or give as gifts. You might also ask the cost of black-and-white prints. If they're considerably less, you can save money by having the photographer shoot a roll to reproduce as gifts.

Videotaping the reception is a costly proposition. For an edited tape, including titles, a still shot of the invitation, and voice-overs, you're into about a thousand dollars for the ceremony alone. To record the reception this way without being obtrusive is almost impossible in an indoor or dark setting, although it is feasible for an outdoor wedding. But is it worth it? Do you really want Aunt Mary interviewed about how glad she is that you finally got married? Without voices, you'll get some dancing, toasting, and the like, but not much else. My advice—don't waste your money. Super-8 movie cameras aren't much better, even though your brother might be dying to try it out for his new film course. Even if he is the next Robert Altman, don't let him experiment with your wedding. The camera will make your guests nervous and maybe even hostile.

13 • Going Away

You don't have to leave at all, especially if the party is in your own house. Said one bride, "It was a wonderful reception, and the fun went on into the wee hours. We finally said good night to the last guest and collapsed into bed. Next morning, we were greeted with breakfast in bed, prepared by my mother and served by Mike's two children."

In more traditional situations, the reception is officially over when the bride and groom leave. This usually happens within an hour after the cake is cut and served. If you want to stay to the very end, pass the word so that guests feel free to leave before you. For receptions held at clubs, catering halls, or hotels, there's probably a time limit on the fun, anyway, so if you dally too long, the proprietor might drop some gentle hints, such as turning off the lights, or worse, charging an overtime fee. Where you do have a time limit, the best man is supposed to track the time and advise you when to slip away.

If you don't want rice or paper rose petals thrown, just tell your bridesmaids and ushers not to provide them. And if you despise the idea of shoes or cans strung from the bumper of your BMW, mention it to your best man and ushers. Also mention that the car's been wired electrically to shock anyone who tries to play with it.

Unless it's more convenient, you don't have to change into getaway clothes. You can leave the way you came, drive home, change, and be on your way.

Where to Spend the Night

If you've been living together for a while, it's silly to think of your wedding night in terms of newfound passion and sexual revelation.

Chances are you'll both be exhausted and in need of some private time and a good night's sleep. If you're romantic, you'll book a reservation in an elegant old hotel where the room service is as good as the late-night movies, which are guaranteed to star Bette Davis. Otherwise, there's nothing wrong with going to your apartment.

You won't have to worry about a place for the night if you're catching a plane or train to get you to some exotic honeymoon spot, but remember that driving a long distance after a wedding is not a great idea. Mixing high emotions and liquor is dangerous.

Honeymoon Clothes

A bride's trousseau used to make sense. Her clothes were part of the dowry provided by her father. The new husband, who was assuming the financial burden of this woman, was off the hook for about a year, or until his bride needed a change of clothes. The modern working-woman might want some new togs to surprise him with, but she'll buy them herself, as she's been doing for years.

Married or otherwise, vacation trips often inspire some new purchases. Get a new bathing suit, or splurge on a ski jacket. If you are going to Paris, take an empty suitcase!

There are no hard-and-fast rules about honeymoon clothes or trousseau purchases. You've traveled before, and you're bound to know what's worn in the Bahamas. If you have any questions about climate or even local custom, consult a travel agent or airline representative.

Ask a friend, relative, or neighbor to pick up your mail, water the plants, feed the cat, and generally check your apartment while you are gone. If you live in a house, get that automatic timer you've been promising yourself, so that the lights go on and off every night. Weddings are visible enough to target you for robbery.

Coming Home

Once you've wound down from your honeymoon, you begin to think, Aha, a return to normalcy. Wrong. It's still a time to share, especially with the family and friends who worked so hard to get it all together. Have a party and enjoy a postmortem with your close friends. A lot of couples wait until the photo prints arrive and plan the party around a "viewing."

If your busy schedules get in the way of a party, or if you just can't face another planning session, be the hosts at a good, cheap restaurant, or better, and spare yourselves the work.

It is thoughtful to plan a special day to visit your parents. You've probably brought them souvenirs from your trip, anyway, and this is a good time to show them the wedding pictures and thank them again for their support. If they live too far away, call them when you get back.

14 · Other Parties

When people make their wedding plans public, friends are apt to respond by throwing a party. From office luncheons, showers, and bachelor parties to the more traditional rehearsal dinner, getting married can mean being the guest of honor at a series of flings, before or after the wedding. Unless you have a very good reason for discouraging these events (you're allergic to wrapping paper), you should graciously accept the offers while guiding your hosts toward simplicity.

Showers

If a friend wants to give you a shower, you shouldn't tell her that you think it's a dumb idea. Nor should you insist on inviting 50 or more people. Thank her for her thoughtfulness, ask her how many people she could accommodate, and then provide her with a guest list. The only rules about showers are the following: (1) mothers and sisters don't give them (it can look like a solicitation for more gifts); (2) if more than one friend or relative wants to host a shower, encourage them to join forces, and if you do accept a second shower, change the guest list so that the same people don't show up for yet another gift-giving evening; and (3) unless the wedding is an intimate affair, don't ask anyone to a prewedding party who isn't invited to the real thing.

Lots of sophisticated brides shun the idea of showers and other traditional parties. This is often not because they don't like the idea, but because they consider themselves undeserving if they're over 30 or have been married before. Well, these events could turn into Tupperware gatherings, but they don't have to. Nor do they have to become financial or time-consuming burdens to friends. One idea is to limit the amount spent on each gift to, say, five dollars, but there's another trend that's becoming popular: the organizers simply ask guests to chip in five or ten dollars, and with that money they buy refreshments and one major gift. The gift can be a place setting of china, crystal, or flatware; bedding or towels; lingerie; or anything else they think the bride really wants. The beauty of this plan is that it eliminates that horrible point of competition in gift giving. We've all experienced that feeling of spending too much or too little, or of finding that most of the other presents were imaginative and humorous, while ours was a boring coffeepot.

With your prompting, a good hostess will put a ceiling on spending and indicate a theme, if there is one. Let's say that you and your fiancé have been living in a house or apartment that is fully furnished. Your butcher block kitchen was completed last year when the Garland stove arrived; the sheeting for the platform bed really did work well with the wallpaper in the bathroom; and your cookbook library is beginning to encroach on nineteenth-century novelists. What, then, could you possibly need and even begin to suggest as an idea for your shower?

Wine. Horticulture (plants, trees). Writing paper, especially if you're changing your name or adding to it. Bath and beauty products (you can always use another bottle of Oil of Olay). Food, such as tins or jars of smoked oysters, special mustards, or other exotica. Anything that's scented (sachets, candles, soaps, potpourri). Needlepoint or other hobby gifts.

It's okay to have him there, too, but then his friends should be asked as well. They can bring a "shower" gift for him, or if you want to challenge everyone's imagination, switch it—let the women shop for him, the men for you. Sometimes these joint showers work beautifully, but often, it's not nearly as relaxed as an "all-girl" affair. I doubt if he'll shed many tears about not being there when you receive that Sabatier knife. Still, it is a good idea to invite him to stop in toward the end of the party to greet the hostess and your friends.

Showers to Avoid

People tie dollar bills—with ribbon to identify the donor—to a plant or tree. It's called a money tree, and it's supposed to be a practical gift for the bride who's moving far away.

In Bridal Bingo, if the bride's name can be spelled in five letters, you can play it by adapting regular bingo. He gets the free space. Need I say more?

Wedding porn has gone beyond Frederick's of Hollywood mail-order items to gifts from the Pleasure Chest. It wasn't funny during the sexual revolution; it isn't funny now.

Bachelor Parties, Bridesmaid Luncheons

The bachelor dinner was originally designed as a farewell to freedom. The groom would invite his attendants to a club or restaurant, give them their gifts, and cry on their shoulders. The bridesmaid luncheon was originally designed as a farewell to virginity. The bride would invite her attendants to a club or restaurant, give them their gifts, and cry on their shoulders while crossing her fingers. This is probably how the war between the sexes was ignited. In any case, you can have lunch, dinner, or anything else with your good friends, singly or together, but it's clearly not a "must."

Professional or Office Parties

At some companies, they call them "pours"—that is, any party, given on behalf of an employee, where the wine and liquor flow. The incentive for these celebrations is usually predicated on some natural rite of passage—retirement, birth, marriage, and especially leaving the company for a better job. Typically, people gather in someone's office during "down time," and with great jocularity and goodwill, the honored guest is toasted, gifted, and occasionally mocked. If you're the guest and none of these people has been invited to the wedding, you don't have to apologize or explain. Your fellow workers are doing this for two major reasons: (1) they like you; and (2) they're desperate for a break in the ordinary office routine. All you have to do is be gracious, go along with it, and send a postcard to all from your honeymoon location.

The Rehearsal Dinner

For simple weddings with a minimum number of attendants, you don't have to have a rehearsal, but for large, formal ceremonies, everyone will be more relaxed if they're coached in advance by the clergyman or officiant. This rehearsal usually takes place in the evening or late afternoon on the day before the wedding and is followed by cocktails and a sit-down or buffet dinner. By the old rules, the groom's parents paid for the dinner, but, as discussed earlier, the financial responsibilities of your wedding can be worked out in other ways.

Whether you rehearse or not, you may want to celebrate the night before with your good friends and parents. And if out-of-town guests have arrived, some of them, if not all, might be included. The only thing you have to watch out for is the party that drags into the night, leaving everyone hung over or exhausted for the wedding. There is nothing wrong with putting a time limit on the revelry, but let an attendant or someone other than the host(s) make the announcement.

Another problem can arise if the ceremony is being held on Sunday. As one bride reported, "It was a marathon weekend of two families being put together who had nothing to say to one another. It would have been much better if it were only Saturday night, plus the wedding on Sunday."

I can recall two different rehearsal dinners, both of which caused some problems. The first was a formal sit-down dinner, held at a private club. Women in long dresses, men in dinner clothes, the whole bit. Toasts were offered and returned, music and dancing were provided, and everyone thanked the groom's parents for hosting such a marvelous party. The problem was that the bride's family didn't have the money to compete with this luxury for the wedding itself, which was a lovely though modest event followed by a short cocktail reception. Everyone concluded that the groom's parents had every intention of outdoing the bride's, thereby hinting that they felt their son was not marrying well. Even if these people didn't intend to hurt feelings, they managed to do so by not adapting to a different social environment. No prewedding party should ever be so elaborate that it outshines the main event. The only time this rule should be broken is if the wedding is strictly a private affair.

The other dinner was in keeping with the wonderful spirit of the couple, their families, and their friends. About fifty people were invited to an evening barbecue, with a menu of homemade roast chicken, sausages, buckets of potato salad, beans, and cole slaw. It was a lot of fun, but a lot of work, and the next day the tension and tiredness showed. Everyone agreed that the caterer should have been asked to at least provide a clean-up staff for the rehearsal dinner.

My advice is to keep this evening small, simple, and as intimate as possible. Remember that attendants' spouses should be invited, as well as the clergyman or officiant. And don't forget that the bride is supposed to return any toasts made to her by her future husband.

15 · The Gifts: Giving and Receiving

Starting from the time people hear about the wedding until a year afterward, unless you specify "no gifts please" on your invitations (and some couples do), you can expect friends and family to send presents. Even remarriages, which etiquette experts say do not require wedding gifts, bring in their fair share of loot. The problem, as always, is minimizing the number of salad bowls you receive and preventing a stampede of white elephants. Ergo, the growing popularity of the bridal gift registry.

Registering Your Choices

If you wind up getting six toasters as wedding presents, it's probably your own fault. Most people turn to the unimaginative toaster either because they don't know you well enough to choose something more personal or because you didn't outline your preferences with a local bridal registry service. If you think the registry is a crass way of soliciting or pressuring people for gifts, you're wrong. All the service does is list your choices, take care of all the paper work, and make sure you receive no more than the eight place settings of flatware you require. They are not provided with a guest list, and they don't threaten to destroy credit ratings if guests don't shop there. The only way a person learns whether you've registered is by asking you, your friends, or your family.

What the store gets from all this work is the profit from the gifts they sell. Nothing more. Guests get a convenient alternative to shopping in the dark, and you get what you want. Before you register, shop together—you both have to live with those patterns. And if you register a silver pattern at, say, $450 a place setting, be sure that's not the only item on your list. Don't forget to inform the registry of any gifts received from other sources so they can cross these things off the list.

Where to Register

You can sign in at more than one store. For example, you may love a crystal pattern at Tiffany's and want everything else from Macy's. Your fiancé's hometown shouldn't be ignored, either. If Macy's has a branch there, they'll coordinate the registry for you. Otherwise, stop in or call in your choices to the registry of a comparable department store in his town.

Aside from the large department stores and specialty shops that cater to brides throughout the country, a lot of small boutiques will provide similar scaled-down services. In Bridgehampton, New York, a store called The Complacent Cook offers a modified service. The bride doesn't register preferences, but the store keeps a list of what's been purchased, thus eliminating duplication. The implication is that anything from this shop will please the bride.

I also know a groom who registered in a similar way at his local hardware store. He was hoping to get some tools for their new house. The proprietor was so pleased with the sales in connection with this wedding that he sent the couple his own gift.

You can ask any small shop if they'll allow you to register. Let's say what you need and want is shrubbery or plants for your new house or apartment. Your florist or nursery will probably make a list of your choices and advise any guests who want to contribute to your landscape. The point is, formal registry services in large stores will offer a great range of gifts in many categories, but the small merchants may have just what you need. Don't overlook them simply because they're specialists.

What to List

I'll never forget telling my mother how silly I thought it was to spend all that money on English bone china when we entertained so casually. That was one marriage and many years ago. Today I find myself entertaining exclusively with the Royal Worcester service for 12 that my mother gave me on the occasion of my second wedding. This may be your only opportunity to get a head start on collecting the finer things in life. Crystal, china, and silver should be among your list of preferences. One tip for registering the high-priced spread: go for the basics—dinner plates rather than cereal bowls; red and white wineglasses rather than decanters. If you get 8 or 10 plates, you can set a fabulous table by using inexpensive glass soup or salad bowls.

In addition to formal dinnerware, registries usually list the following: stainless steel flatware; casual barware; casual dinnerware (often oven-to-table); cooking equipment (pots and pans); kettles; coffee makers; appliances (food processors, vacuum cleaners); kitchen equipment (knives, colanders, spice racks, clocks); linens (blankets, towels, sheets, tablecloths); and entertainment items (radios, TVs, stereos, tapes).

If the store's standard gift list does not, for example, extend to sporting goods and you would love to have an Exercycle, list it on a separate sheet which the store will provide.

In the old days, most wedding linens and silver were monogrammed. If you are changing your name and you like the idea of personalized towels, give your initials to the registrar. Your last name initial is large and centered, surrounded by smaller first and middle or maiden name initials. If you are keeping your maiden name, don't consider it.

Money

There's nothing wrong with spreading the words that gifts of cash would be appreciated, especially if you are going to move or plan to be in transit for a while. Couples who are saving for a down payment on a car or other big item may be twice as grateful for a check.

If the bride and groom have an already furnished home, people often give gift certificates, stocks, or bonds. They should be made out in both names (Joan Smith and Richard Davis), unless it's clear that the bride is changing hers after the wedding. The most creative certificate I've heard of was a $100 gift, good at any Exxon station.

Chipping In

Some friends, knowing full well that all you really want is a color TV, will pool their resources to provide it. These are thoughtful people, and they deserve special applause for their consideration.

New Ideas for Gifts

Electronics

Atari, Intellivision setups and cassettes.
Calculators, hand-held electronic games.
Telephones.
Telephone answering machines.
Cassette recorders, including the Sony Walkman with two earphone sets.
Cameras or camera equipment (projectors, prepaid film processing).
Car stereos.
TV remote control hookups.

Home Security

Smoke alarms, automatic light switches.
Escape ladders and a Captain Kelly fire extinguisher.
Burglar alarms.
Window gates.

Collector's Items (from a reputable shop that will allow an exchange)

Antique maps, framed.
First editions.
A piece of old porcelain.
Antique table linen.
Sculpture, paintings, etchings, lithographs.
An old quilt.
Tapestries and rugs to hang.

Spectator Sports

Two tickets to the Superbowl.
A box seat at the stadium.
Theater tickets for the opera, a repertory company, the philharmonic.
Fifty dollars worth of rides at the local amusement park.

Edibles

A gift basket of gourmet foods prepared by a pro.

A gift basket designed by the giver.

Breakfast in bed for a month of Sundays, catered, delivered on trays at 11:00 A.M. along with the newspaper.

Dinner for two at a fabulous restaurant.

Potables

Wines, brandies, liqueurs.

A year's supply of Beck's beer, one case each month, and a bottle of champagne on the first anniversary.

Horticulture

Trees, plants, shrubs.

Permanent arrangements of silk or dried flowers.

Etiquette Notes

Displaying your gifts. This is an old custom which many people consider ostentatious and materialistic. The modest gift is always dwarfed by the showy one, and the presentation really reduces the wedding to the "honor of your presents." If your good friends want to see what you got, you can show them a few of your favorite things, privately.

Damaged presents. If you receive wineglasses that are chipped, go to the store and arrange for an even exchange. If the gift is from an out-of-town shop, call the consumer service department and they'll tell you how to get a replacement. If the gift was mailed to you and not insured, don't call the giver. Just get out the Krazy Glue and hope for the best.

Exchanges. If you really want to exchange something and can do it without the giver knowing, go ahead. But don't let Aunt Alice think that her ashtrays were a poor choice.

The Gifts You Give

You and your fiancé don't have to give each other wedding gifts. For some couples, their rings are their presents to each other. Others will find some smaller token to give when the excitement dies down. But pragmatists, if there's any fun money left, will spend it jointly on something they need.

Your attendants deserve a remembrance of the occasion, which you may choose to monogram. Honor attendants can have slightly more elaborate gifts, if you like.

Only you know your friends well enough to find the perfect present, but for bridesmaids you may consider the following: earrings, lockets, pins, bracelets, or other jewelry; picture frames, leather-bound diaries, makeup cases, billfolds; crystal atomizers, silver comb holders, porcelain pencil cups, mirrored makeup trays; credit-card sized calculators.

Ushers might be given cuff links, tie clips, money clips, belt buckles, wallets, leather-bound diaries, fancy ball-point pens, porcelain shaving mugs and brushes, or credit-card sized calculators.

If your parents went to a lot of time and expense to get your wedding off the ground, they deserve some kind of gift, even though they won't be expecting one. They'd probably love a photograph of the two of you, framed in silver, rattan, fabric, or leather.

I heard about a couple who sent their parents singing telegrams the day after the wedding. Such companies as the Music Box or Eastern Onion will write a special thank-you song if you provide them with information about the people being thanked. It's a great way to surprise them and show your love and appreciation.

Parents will especially love a letter, even a sentimental one, expressing your feelings about them and your new life. Your mother will probably wrap it in plastic and keep it with your first grade report card.

Thank-You Notes

Gifts were once sent to the bride's parents' home. Today they go to the couple's home or to his or her apartment. Here's where the sexual revolution pays off: you both get to write thank-you notes! After you record each gift (see chapter 2), write a note as soon as possible. If you let it all pile up, you'll have a problem. There's an art to writing these notes and making people feel that their gifts were special, wanted, and appreciated. If you are the one who is writing, include your fiancé's or husband's name in the body of the note, and vice versa. Here are some examples:

Dear Aunt Margaret,

Thank you for the expertly etched crystal vase. John and I are so inspired by it that we're starting to grow our own supply of flowers from the new cutting garden. We hope you'll be able to see it soon, in all its glory.

Love,

Dear Mr. and Mrs. Jones,

Sandra and I think of ourselves as a truly modern couple, sharing responsibilities like housekeeping and cooking. But if it weren't for your terrific electric wok, I doubt if I could hold up my end of the bargain. Chicken and almonds is the specialty of the house—I hope you'll come for dinner and sample it soon.

Best regards,

Even if you're not enthusiastic about the door chimes that play "Here Comes the Bride," you should make an effort to be gracious.

Dear Mike,

John said he always wanted me to feel like a bride, and I bet he confided in you. The chimes will never let me forget our wonderful wedding and the very special affection we have for friends like you.

We hope to be in Salem soon. We'll ring your bell when we get there.

Love,

Money gifts and gift certificates are handled differently. Don't mention the amount; do mention how you plan to spend it.

Dear Sylvia and Pete,

Thank you for your generous wedding check. John and I have

been saving for an oriental carpet, and your gift means we can buy the Bokhara we fell in love with.

See you at the wedding.

Love,

Joint gifts from friends or relatives should be acknowledged individually. Even though each letter may be similar, they should not be identical. If the gift was from a group—e.g., friends at the office—one letter sent to "everyone" is fine.

Really big weddings, involving more than two hundred expected presents, allow bride and groom to send out printed acknowledgment cards, followed as soon as possible by a personal thank-you. They might read as follows:

Janice Wilson and Thomas Stewart
wish to acknowledge
the receipt of your lovely wedding gift
and will write a personal note of thanks
at an early date

If you wait more than four weeks to write, it's a little insulting. And it is better to use your own personal stationery instead of greeting card thank-yous with wedding bells on the flap.

16 · Whose Paintings Hang on the Wall?

It might have been love at first sight for you and Ken, but his chrome, glass, and leather furniture took an instant dislike to your quilted chintz sofas. If you think it's going to be easy to agree on what to get rid of and what to keep, you may be in for a nasty shock. For some couples who bring substantial material dowries to their marriages, joining possessions is more than a simple decorating problem—it's a struggle for power. And whoever wins the battle of the wing chair could lose the marriage. Sound ridiculous? Here's what one woman told me: "My husband had a master's degree in industrial design, and he thought it made him an authority on furniture. He loved Danish modern and wanted everything paneled in walnut. I loved overstuffed sofas and Victoriana. Our solution was to get divorced."

The fights people have about furniture are usually not about furniture at all. They're about keeping control for fear of losing the last vestige of identity to the greater glory of "us." That ugly table may have some personal historical value, even though Parke-Bernet wouldn't give it a tumble. Or a small knickknack can cause trouble if it has heavy symbolic associations for one partner and seems a simple piece of junk to the other.

Many couples claim that merging households is a good test of marital compatibility. Try to get all the domestic hassles out of the way before you marry, and sign the lease before the license. The first step in this highly sensitive area of negotiation is deciding where to live.

The ideal is to start out in a brand-new place with as much space as you can afford. If you've lived alone for a while, it's tough to share a one-bedroom apartment that has no extra room to give you the privacy you're used to having. Those extra rooms could also take care of a lot of other problems. If he's passionate about hunting scenes (which you hate), or you want to duplicate an Oscar de la Renta room with floral printed draperies (which he hates), you can find a solution without constantly offending each other. Another reason to start off fresh is to eliminate the psychological ghosts of former marriages or affairs that can haunt an old apartment. Remarried couples might want a totally different environment from what they had in their first marriages. If she had a suburban split-level, she might want to renovate a barn. Or he might have acquired a distaste for high-rise living, choosing a loft instead. Knowing what you both need physically (space for office, children, etc.) and emotionally (light rooms, a view, security) is the first step to successfully finding and sharing living space.

Admittedly, a new place is an extravagance that many can't afford. The alternative is for one of you to move in with the other. It can work, but an awful lot of compromises will have to be made along the way. Aside from two households of furniture that must be stored, sold, or integrated, your greatest challenge will be sharing the closets and medicine chests. You may think you are one of those people who could take off tomorrow for parts unknown and fit everything into your van. But I bet your closets come close to filling a jumbo jet. Even if you send the yearbooks and the incomplete Scrabble games back to mother's, you'll never fit him in. Weed it all out and store it, or give it away. And if that doesn't work, buy an armoire, or hire a carpenter to build another closet.

Some couples keep a small city apartment in order to put most of their resources into a second home. This plan solves a lot of problems, since two vegetable peelers are essential. All the extra beds, furniture, and accessories can be used in the country, even if it's just a temporary decorating scheme.

If either of you has children, don't shake them up too much with major plans to redecorate. Kids don't like change, especially if it's all happening at once. Suzanne and Dave had been married three years before they decided to move. From the beginning, his girls had had their own room, which Suzanne had decorated with cheerful wallpaper and fun furniture. When the children learned about the move, they were miserable. With a lot of effort, Suzanne found 12 rolls of the same wallpaper (which had been discontinued) and duplicated the decoration. Her reason: "Divorced children live in so many places until the parents get settled again that any change in their living space could be traumatic. When the kids saw their new room, a line-for-line copy of the old one, they started to love the whole house."

The first step in the big merge is to inventory everything you both own. When the lists are complete, mark the things that stay and the things that go. If your cup runneth over with double everything, follow this formula: keep the best, get rid of the rest, and avoid an "early boy-meets-girl" decorating mishmash.

Fine furniture, rugs, art collections, electronic equipment, antiques, and the like should not be sold or given away unless you are absolutely sure they won't increase in value. A lot of people invest in these objects as hedges against inflation, especially since the art and antique markets have consistently set new records at auction. If these items can't fit into your place now, store them.

Estimate the number of shelves needed to accommodate books and records. For some people these items make up the bulk of their possessions. Build the bookshelves before moving in so that you don't have to live with stacks of cartons for a year.

Personal or professional papers might need to be moved out of a clothes closet and into a filing cabinet. You can usually pick up these cabinets secondhand or at a discount from an office supply company.

Kitchen space can be dramatically increased if you install wall grids that hang utensils or pots and pans. If cabinets are still inadequate, place extra dishes and barware in a trunk that doubles as a side or cocktail table.

Figuring out what to keep or get rid of can be complicated. When emotions get charged, you may have to call in an arbitrator. In this case, that person ought to be a professional decorator or interior designer. In refreshing deadpan style, he or she will evaluate the space and what you own in relation to how you live. If you do a lot of entertaining, for example, an adequate conversation area will be designed for, say, a dozen people. If you paint or play music as a sideline, space will be set aside to accommodate those interests.

The decorator may advise getting rid of more things than you planned and may also suggest acquiring some brand-new items. But if you both love the red parson's table, and the decorator wants it donated to Goodwill, find another decorator.

What to Do with Unwanted Stuff

No matter how you come to terms with planning your home, you'll have to account for the unwanted items. There are several ways to do this.

Storage. You can pay a storage company to come in and pack everything, insure it, and store it at their warehouse. In large metropolitan areas, this can be expensive. In suburban and rural places, it's relatively cheap. The advantage is that you don't have to bother wrapping table legs or covering mattresses, let alone hiring a U-Haul and risking a ruptured disc. Storage companies usually charge by the cubic foot rather than by weight. Some will charge you the greater of the two values. A reputable company will give free moving and storage estimates. The monthly rental fee, by the way, is peanuts compared to the packing and moving costs. Again, you'll pay the higher charge when you retrieve your shipment.

If someone has offered an attic or basement where you can move and store everything yourselves, plan carefully. No matter how dry a basement seems, books, wood furniture, mattresses, and pillows should be well wrapped in plastic to avoid mold or mildew. Also, don't place anything (except table legs) directly on a basement floor. Nail boards together and make a platform, or place objects on an aluminum table.

Don't accept an attic offer until you look over the space. If you have to haul furniture up a tiny staircase that starts from a shallow platform, be sure you'll be able to turn the corner with the couch.

Yard, garage, tag, apartment, and loft sales. In suburban and rural areas, you may need to get a license and pay a small fee in order to have any commercial activity in a residential area. A lot of people place signs on telephone poles at major intersections or take out ads in their local newspapers to announce a yard sale. If you don't think you have enough merchandise to hold your own, get together with neighbors or friends and pool your resources.

You can have the same kind of sale in a city, but getting the word around might not be so easy. Post an announcement in the lobby of your building or in the elevator or mailbox area. If the lobby is loaded with stuffed shirts, the laundry room might be a better place. Company newsletters or house organs are also good advertising vehicles, especially since there's no charge. City dwellers can also join forces for a tag sale at an apartment or a loft; if you do, it's best to stick with people in your own building.

Auctions. If you have quite a bit of merchandise, you could hold an auction in your house or apartment by hiring a licensed auctioneer who gets a certain percentage of the take. The auctioneer will come to your house, evaluate the items, and determine if it's worth getting involved at all. Some place ads for you and take the cost out of your profits. Others will ask you to place the ad yourself. And it is still a good idea to notify friends or neighbors independently.

Private auction houses work a little differently. The most exclusive ones, such as Sotheby, Parke-Bernet, and Christie's, don't handle "households" unless you're a Du Pont. What they'll do is agree to offer your Picasso lithograph at one of their print auctions. Over a period of a year, they'll sell everything from rugs to furniture, but since their clients are specialists, they want their merchandise coded accordingly. Other auction houses will take roomfuls of furniture and the like and sell it by lot or item. If you're really curious about how it works, go to an auction or two. You may even find the perfect table to go with his easy chair.

Charitable contributions. Giving things to your impoverished brother is not considered a deductible contribution by the IRS. The Salvation Army, Goodwill Industries, religious organizations, accredited schools, and tax-exempt foundations, to name a few, qualify in the eyes of the agents. Such organizations will assess the value of the goods, itemize each piece, and give you a receipt stating the dollar total. The IRS is the last word on legitimate charities, and you should check with them before turning everything over to Joe Schmoe's Home for Wayward Men.

Lending things to friends in need. One bride advised, "If your husband cares a lot about something you just can't live with, persuade him to lend it out because you'll never see it again." If you're not that devious and really want to help out a friend, think again. People are funny about things they live with, even if they reside at the Hyatt Hotel. After a while, a kind of "squatter's rights" mentality takes over and the Chinese chifforobe becomes theirs, not yours. Try asking for it when your first child is born, and you may get, "Gee, Sally, if I'd known you wanted it back, I wouldn't have decorated the whole room around it." The message is—either give it away or find another solution.

Giving things away. If your family and friends aren't interested, and you don't care about a tax write-off, instead of throwing things in the garbage, find a youth club or inner-city organization that can use what you've got. A ratty old couch could solve a lot of decorating problems for a campus club.

Day-care centers might need some extra bedding or sheets, or a senior citizens' home could use that Ping-Pong table. Of course, charity can begin a lot closer to home. Maybe the lounge at your health club is a candidate for solid leftovers. Or why not redo your office? Just because the walls are flexible doesn't mean you can't hang your etchings on them.

17 · Money and the Law

Nobody wants to think of marriage as a financial merger, but, unless one of you is independently wealthy, it is almost impossible to survive double-digit inflation and still hang onto what's left of the American dream without the benefit of two incomes. Today, over 57 percent of all women between the ages of twenty and sixty-four work outside the home, and the traditional family unit, where the husband is the sole breadwinner, has shrunk to 17 percent. The result is that modern couples work out their finances and legal entanglements with the same attention they give to their wedding plans.

It is no secret that one out of three marriages ends in divorce. But the emotional pain of separation might be a drop in the bucket compared to the long-range effects of a property settlement that turns sunny optimists into bitter defeatists. To avoid this kind of potential heartache, couples who expect their marriages to last a lifetime are managing their money with the kind of pragmatism they would bring to a business.

Experts agree that the first step toward financial compatibility is knowing what you both have in money and property—a full disclosure breakdown. Next, you must decide what you own independently or in common.

Premarital Financial Agreements

If you have any doubts or premonitions about what might happen to your Beatles record collection should you divorce or separate, consider having an antenuptial agreement drawn up by your lawyer.

A lot of people dismiss them as antiromantic or a kind of self-fulfilling prophesy. Others find comfort in the knowledge that, should a divorce occur, everything they worked for over the years won't find its way into somebody else's life. Originally, these contracts were a protection against gold diggers who wanted to profit from an early divorce. Today, they're a protection against medieval divorce laws. If one partner can prove ignorance of what was being signed, some of these agreements won't hold up in court; however, most cases are honored as written.

A typical agreement, based on the termination of the marriage through divorce or death, states the following: (1) anything owned before the marriage remains the property of that individual (an inventoried list of household items, cars, bank accounts, stocks and bonds, real estate, etc., is written into the agreement); (2) all properties or assets acquired during the marriage will be owned jointly (unless otherwise stipulated in separate agreements); (3) in the event of a divorce, alimony will be paid to the spouse based on an agreed percentage of income or salary for a specific period of time, and no longer; (4) if there are children, the couple will make every effort to obtain joint custody and share in their support; and (5) in the event of death, rather than divorce, the estate (including all insurance) will be distributed in a specific way.

For couples who have no beef with their state divorce laws, a simple property agreement or inventory of who owned what before marriage might suffice. Still, no matter how frightened or gun-shy people are, most don't want to sign anything in connection with their marriage but the license.

As one groom explained, "I guess I can understand some contracts, but I think you can poison a relationship by assuming the terms of its end." Another agreed: "If Audrey and I couldn't trust each other, we wouldn't have married. I don't always want to look over my shoulder when we spend money. We have an unwritten agreement that if we split, whatever we accumulated during the marriage will be shared. Whatever was ours before is ours alone."

Managing Money

Experts advise a kind of separate but equal approach to the purse strings. According to lawyer Peter Bronstein, "The more you mingle assets, the more you risk losing your share of the investment through death or divorce." This means separate checking and savings accounts, as well as individual names on stocks, bonds, or other financial holdings.

Experts also advise setting up a fair system of paying the bills. Some couples have an "I'll pay this month, you pay next" strategy for rent or mortgage, utility, and food bills. But Jane Bryant Quinn, a professional financial adviser, told *Money* magazine, "I know some households where the husband borrows from the wife if his expenses run over budget one month. Then she says, 'You owe me.' That's not the way a marriage should work. When you say, 'these are your bills,' and 'these are my bills,' you run the risk of quibbling unnecessarily over money. It should all go into one pot, regardless of who's making more and who's making less."

Carl and Gloria, who have been married for three years, agree. "Carl used to be adamant about 'my money' or 'your money'—but never 'our money,' " explained Gloria. "Nothing was shared, and he always wanted to know, 'Is this yours or mine?' in case we split up. I was much more committed to the idea of staying together, and with time, he felt the same way. Now we pool our income."

But you don't have to have a joint checking account to have a successful marriage. One couple with a city apartment and a country house simply split the difference. She pays all the expenses in town, and he pays all the expenses on the house, which they own jointly.

Another advantage of separate ownership is estate taxes. *Money* magazine says, "The IRS taxes jointly held properties in the estate of the first to die, unless the survivor can prove he or she contributed at least a portion of the money that went to pay for it. But as a rule, with separate ownership, only assets in the deceased's name are taxed." Since the law gives a marital deduction of $250,000, you won't pay any tax on an estate valued at $500,000 if half or more of it was in your name.

Investments

Whether it's a first or second marriage, couples usually pool some of their resources to invest in the future. Some expect to have children and want to be able to finance a family without totally changing their way of living. Others want to educate the children they've got. An investment counselor offers this advice: "Know what you want your money to do (i.e., capitalize your own business, support your retirement, or be used as a down payment on a house), and seek out the sources who can advise you." But, he cautions, financial specialists aren't available to everyone. "If you had $10,000 to play with, virtually no specialist would talk to you. One percent is the average management fee, and since a simple business letter actually costs fifteen dollars to send, it's not worth the time."

You can, however, turn to other sources. If you're in a middle-income bracket, use your company's personnel facilities to investigate retirement, pension, social security benefits, profit sharing, and medical and life insurance plans. Or go to the wealth of how-to investment books that can offer the kind of information and guidance you need. If you have a lot of money, get good referrals. Use your friends' contacts, and don't be afraid to ask specific questions. If you're dealing with a lawyer, find out what he'll charge and what he'll do for you. "Lawyers are like art galleries—they don't like to talk about prices, but they charge a lot," a broker said.

Real estate and money funds are good investments and hedges against inflation. The value of a house has been increasing at a higher annual percentage than inflation, and interest on a bank mortgage is tax deductible. Bank certificates can also yield good interest. And some marketing funds or stock investments make perfect tax shelters.

Even though junior might join the merchant marines instead of going to college, you can provide for his higher education anyway. Consider establishing a trust fund, earmarked for the child's education. The tax benefits on the interest are in your favor. Einstein once said that the greatest invention of modern man is compound interest. In the case of trust funds, the interest is credited to the trust, and since the child earns no income, he pays no taxes. Children can be a natural tax shelter.

Before making any major decisions about investments, get the advice of a professional tax accountant. He'll review your combined income and help you decide how to come up with the kind of investments that will help you fight the disastrous effects of the marriage tax.

The Marriage Tax

A few years ago, single people lobbied for a more equitable tax scale. They said they were being penalized because they weren't married, and they were right. The tax schedules were quite unfair. To everyone's surprise (and possibly because an official of the IRS was contemplating a divorce) the singles had their wishes incorporated into a Tax Reform Act.

But along with reform in favor of singles came discrimination toward married couples who work and earn similar incomes. All of a sudden it became profitable to "live in sin," and cohabitation was touted as the best way to beat the marriage tax. Other couples had a different approach—the fiscal divorce. Their plan was to divorce at the end of each calendar year and remarry at the beginning of the next. Even at $1,000 a shot, the divorce saved some people close to $4,000 on their taxes.

Once the IRS caught on to the much-publicized scheme, they argued that "divorce in contemplation of remarriage and continued cohabitation is flouting the law." They want couples to file jointly til death do them part. Also, the Supreme Court recently refused to hear a case challenging the absurdity of the marriage tax, and nuptial bliss was dealt a heavy blow.

There's a movement afoot in Congress, championed by New Jersey representative Millicent Fenwick. She and others are trying to make it optional for couples to file jointly as singles, so that people aren't forced to lie, cheat, or give up the idea of marriage altogether. First marriages might be pinched by the marriage tax, but remarriages, already under financial strain, suffer more.

Remarried Money: Double Trouble

Life had become absurd. After twelve years and two children, his marriage was being reduced to a balance sheet of assets and liabilities, money and property. Accountants and lawyers were indeed taking over the world, he thought, giving a market value to love, pain, ideas, and dreams. His private life finally had a bottom line—the result of seedy little strangers reviewing the profit and loss factors of his marriage.

He tried to put the idea out of his mind, knowing that it meant financial suicide. But the image grew to an obsession every time the 6:27 pulled out of the station. Once he even laughed aloud as commuter eyebrows lifted in unison. Maybe it was clause 27-A in the separation agreement that finally did it. The next day, he hired a group of industrial carpenters to saw his $150,000 suburban house in half.

"It was the act of a madman," the papers said. They called it a modern-day version of King Solomon's threat to cut the baby in half to determine the real mother. To others, this man was a hero. Why? He had the courage to symbolically challenge the financial brutality of divorce.

Like sex, money is a primary source of tension in marriage. Recent reports claim that 54 percent of all couples fight about money. And when cash is limited, the figures swell to 64 percent. Many divorced people still wince when they think about the money factor in their first marriages. In some cases, money symbolized the psychological dynamic of the relationship. If the husband was the only income producer, he became the providing father, and the wife became his child. Others faced the ongoing trauma of measuring their self-worth by what they earned. Few would ever again ignore the fact that money has the power to make or break a relationship.

"If I had analyzed my second marriage as if it were a business deal, I never would have done it," said a thirty-six-year-old stockbroker. His new wife not only lost her alimony payments, but her earned income put them in a higher tax bracket. "We needed a larger apartment for the kids, and for a while, I didn't think we could make it financially," he explained. "But our life together is more important than the money it takes to finance it. Deciding to marry isn't like choosing a good commodity. If it were, we'd be obscenely rich in emotional happiness."

For older couples, social security benefits are reduced when they marry, and many choose cohabitation as an alternative. Others, who wish to protect complicated estate holdings for their heirs or family members, have to shell out exorbitant sums in legal fees when they remarry. According to Peter Bronstein, "Many relationships that flourish in the early stages can collapse under the financial strain of remarriage. People don't bother to find out if what they're giving up is worth what they're getting."

But remarriage can be economically beneficial. Sharing the costs of housing, food, and entertainment doesn't mean that two can live as cheaply as one, but it helps. The idea, as always, is to discuss money and finances as pragmatically and unemotionally as possible. Cutting off that dialogue can harm your chances of adjusting to a difficult phenomenon—the outlay of cash to another family.

Alimony and Child Support

"I wouldn't consider marrying again," said an attractive thirty-five-year-old woman who is a doctor. "Most of the eligible men are divorced and loaded down with alimony and child support. Why should I work for another woman?"

When Virgil said that "love conquers all," he probably didn't figure on a second wife's attitude toward alimony and child support. Nor did he realize that the average divorced man is living on half of his former income. One man, a clothing contractor, has been divorced from his first wife for ten years. Two of his three children attend private schools. His new wife also has three children, one of whom is still supported by her first husband.

"I'm afraid I made the mistake of thinking that my first wife would be ethical and honorable about money when we divorced," he confessed. "But when she started to gouge, my lawyer suggested that I put the bulk of the money in alimony. His theory was that because she was young and attractive, she'd remarry. But I had no such luck."

Another man, a remarried writer, said, "In most cases, alimony is an outrage. If the law demanded proof of need until a woman was on her feet, it would be different, but right now, it's used punitively to get back at the mate."

From the man's point of view, the high cost of alimony can sap his discretionary money, forcing him to seek other sources of income. "My work has taken a turn I wouldn't have chosen," said the contractor. "I'm accepting jobs that I'd like to reject. I guess you sell out directly in relation to your alimony settlement."

But a man's conflict and hardship caused by his divorce settlement is small potatoes compared to how his new wife feels. Directly or indirectly, the second wife is giving part of her income to another woman. Almost all remarried women whose husbands pay alimony express one common emotion—anger.

Cathy and Mark left their first marriages to be together. She works, and she accepted no alimony. But Mark paid a high premium for his freedom. "I don't really resent the alimony," said Cathy. "Long ago I realized that if Mark and I wanted to be together, we'd have to pay for it. I'm lucky to have him at any price. But I do object to the law. I resent the fact that a healthy woman is allowed to rape a man financially. I think it's horrid that I was eligible for alimony even though I was working."

Betty and Ken have been remarried for two years. "I'm still angry at Ken's first wife for manipulating him," said Betty, "and I resent working to pay her alimony. What really gets me is that she's insincere—espousing feminist lines while continuing to bitch about her poverty."

Child support is usually a slightly less volatile issue for a remarried couple. No one seems to blame the children for the parents' mistakes. But problems of stepparenting and accepting the new family setup can cause resentment about money. "I wouldn't mind spending money on the kids if their mother didn't undermine my position all the time," Betty continued. "In fact, if I could deal with the kids on neutral grounds, I'd probably give more in every way."

How do remarried couples survive these problems? They're diminished in large measure because of the lack of shock value. Debts of alimony or child support were conditions that existed before remarriage, and unless the man is a pathological liar, his new wife knew what to expect. Paying off a settlement is not like coming home and announcing that you've lost your job or that the house burned down. There's no real dramatic impact. It's just there until the kids grow up or until the alimony can be contested.

The alimony law grew out of a particular conception of male-female relationships. It assumed that wives were dependent properties without the wit or means to survive by themselves. It also assumed that women would never choose to end their marriages and therefore deserved some compensation for being "wronged." But the more society discards these notions, the more the law is apt to change.

According to some state laws, a man can petition for lower alimony payments under the following conditions: (1) if the woman is working; (2) if she is living with a man; or (3) if her alimony and child support payments were lumped together and the children are no longer eligible for support. Also, in the recent precedent-setting case of *Carter* v. *Carter,* the court upheld that, if both parents have their own incomes, a wife and husband are equally responsible for child support.

On the other hand, remarriage doesn't allow a reduction of responsibilities toward a former spouse. Lawyers explain that if the first wife applies for an increase in alimony, the court is not supposed to consider the fact that the husband is remarried, although it happens. If a person were smart enough not to sign an escalation clause, he or she might be off the hook in terms of increased payments.

As one husband summed it up: "When my wife tried to get her alimony increased on the basis of inflation, it didn't work. I learned that the only defense I have against her is an empty bank account."

Does Your Lawyer Make House Calls?

A new phenomenon has occurred in middle-class America: lawyers, once the servants of the very rich and powerful, are advising the working classes on a variety of financial and legal matters. Divorce used to be the first time one would contact a lawyer. Today, marriage can be the incentive. Aside from advising about money, property, wills, credit, and investments, lawyers are handling a brand new area of married life—marriage contracts. A marriage contract can include anything from whether the man and woman will retain or change their names to stipulations about who does the housework and takes out the garbage. Couples are writing in clauses about whether or not they intend to have children and who is responsible for birth control. Right-to-work options for dual-career couples who do have children are also etched in stone. People have been known to specify the number of visits to in-laws during the course of a year, or to promise to give up smoking or drinking.

In his book, *Oh Promise Me but Put It in Writing,* attorney Paul Ashley argues that pragmatism, not romance, is the key to a successful marriage. He thinks that if couples force themselves to think through the decisions they'll face later, they'll avoid the conflicts that traditionally break up marriages.

Contract critics claim that these documents do nothing for a marriage, but a lot for the legal establishment, which benefits from the fees. There's no evidence that marriage contracts—which legislate behavior and pin down life's options—either harm or help. Only you can decide if signing on the dotted line will bring you closer to a fiftieth anniversary.

Marriage Contracts

Following are two examples of the kind of marriage contracts that are being written today.

Contract I

Marriage Contract

We, ______ and ______ , about to enter into a marriage relationship solemnized under the laws of the State of Ohio, have together drafted this Marriage Contract in order to define mutually agreed upon rights and obligations consistent with the goals of our marital relationship. We recognize that these rights and obligations may differ from the traditional rights and obligations of married persons in this State which would prevail in the absence of this Contract. It is our desire that where such differences exist, the provisions of this Contract shall take precedence.

We agree that the prime goal of our marriage shall be mutual and independent growth, both personal and professional. We also agree that neither party shall in any way dominate the marital relationship without the consent of the other, or in any way damage or thwart the growth of the other.

Therefore, in consideration of our mutual promises to marry one another, the mutual promises expressed herein and in consideration of our love and affection for each other, the sufficiency of all the foregoing being hereby acknowledged by both parties, we agree that the provisions herein shall govern our marriage relationship.

ARTICLE I: CAREERS AND DOMICILE

It is agreed that the choice of marital domicile shall be mutual. (Husband) hereby waives any right he may have to determine the legal domicile of the parties.

We agree that a move to another city, whether inside or outside of this State, will not be undertaken unless it appears that the contemplated new locality will offer career opportunities for both the parties, and the likelihood of maintaining a mutually acceptable standard of living. Factors to be considered are the probable income of both parties, the cost of living in the new location, and the extent to which we may desire to deplete previously acquired assets. However, either party may waive the right to continued career opportunity when it appears to that party that the opportunities for the other party outweigh any personal detriment and will, on the whole, be beneficial to the marriage relationship.

The parties also agree that either of us may live separate from the other, outside the city of the marital domicile, for a reasonable period of time, if educational or career requirements or opportunities are presented to one of us at a time when the other, for similar reasons, must remain at the current domicile. It is agreed that such a temporary separation shall in no way alter the marriage relationship, nor shall it constitute a ground for separation or divorce under the laws of Ohio or of any other state.

ARTICLE II: MARITAL HARMONY

It is our mutual desire that disagreements between us should be resolved as quickly as possible with as little distress as possible. We both also desire that the marriage should not terminate unless both of us have earnestly attempted to reconcile serious differences over a reasonable length of time.

Therefore, we agree that a material disagreement between us which is not resolved within a reasonable period of time, or which causes great emotional distress to either party, shall be cause to seek counseling from a professional source. Each of us agrees that the other may seek counseling independently, but that either of us will also attend counseling sessions if requested to do so by the other, or by the counselor.

We further agree that no divorce or separation shall be contemplated unless there are irreconcilable differences or problems, and until a waiting period of two years shall have passed. During that time, we each agree to do whatever can be done to resolve the problems. We agree that professional counseling shall be a prerequisite to any suit for divorce or separation, and that no suit shall be filed until both of us are certain that differences cannot, by any reasonable expectation, be resolved to our mutual satisfaction.

Should counseling be ineffective and the marriage prove to be beyond reconciliation, then, because neither of us desires to cause the other unnecessary emotional distress, each of us waives the right to contest a suit for divorce or separation when filed by the other.

ARTICLE III: CHILDREN

We presently plan to have two children, but we both desire that we shall not have children until approximately six to eight years after the date of our marriage. It is agreed that the decision to have children shall be a mutual one.

It is further agreed that if either of us should be unable to produce children, adoption would be a satisfactory alternative method of having a family.

ARTICLE IV: PROPERTY

Each of us has fully disclosed to the other all properties and assets owned before the marriage, as well as all debts and financial obligations. We desire that all our assets shall be pooled into a common fund, with each of us having full access to the entire amount thereof, without regard to its source. It is agreed, therefore, that all property owned before the marriage, except any which may be held in trust for third persons, and all after-acquired property, whether real or personal, and all other income from any source, as between us, shall be joint property, with the exception, however, of property received, inherited, or purchased by either party which is distinctly personal in its nature, which shall be the sole property of the intended owner.

It is further agreed that both parties shall actively participate in planning the budgeting and distribution of our resources, and that neither of us shall make substantial expenditures nor commitments of resources unless mutually agreed upon.

The parties agree that each will establish his or her own credit as to third persons, and that neither will be responsible for the debts of the other.

We recognize that one of us, in the interest of mutual harmony, may forfeit an educational or career opportunity in order to further such opportunity for the other. We further recognize that such sacrifice may result in a lifetime of impaired earning power. Therefore, it is agreed that if we should be separated or divorced, all property is to be evenly divided between us, with an allowance, however, to compensate for any such actual diminished earning capacity.

It is further agreed that, except for the division of property as described above, neither party shall have any obligation for the support or maintenance of the other after separation or divorce, except to the extent required because of the incapacity of either of us to become self-supporting.

The foregoing shall in no way alter the rights of the spouse who has custody of any of the couple's children to receive support payments for such children.

ARTICLE V: EFFECTS OF THIS CONTRACT

We agree that actions by either of us which are construed by the other as a substantial violation of a material provision of this contract shall constitute "gross neglect of duty" and "extreme cruelty" according to the divorce laws of the State of Ohio.

We also agree that if any part of this contract should be held void or unenforceable for any reason, the remainder of this contract shall nevertheless continue in force and be binding upon us, to the fullest extent permissible under the law.

ARTICLE VI: ALTERATION OR TERMINATION OF CONTRACT

We agree that at least every two years, on or about the even-numbered anniversaries of our marriage, both the terms of this contract and the relationship existing within our marriage shall be reviewed, and altered or amended as deemed necessary.

This contract may be amended or terminated by mutual consent at any time. Amendments, modifications, or alterations of any kind must be in writing and be signed by both parties.

IN WITNESS WHEREOF. . . . .

Contract II

Recitals of Intention

_____ and _____ desire to enter into a marriage relationship, duly solemnized under the laws of the State of _____, the rights and obligations of which relationship differ from the traditional rights and obligations of married persons in the State of _____ which would prevail in the absence of this contract. The parties have together drafted this marriage contract in order to define a marriage relationship sought by the parties which preserves and promotes their individual identities as a man and a woman contracting to live together for mutual benefit and growth.

_____ and _____ are of sound mind and body, have a clear understanding of the terms of this contract and of the binding nature of the agreements contained herein; they freely and in good faith choose to enter into this marriage contract and fully intend it to be legally binding upon themselves.

Now, therefore, in consideration of their affection and esteem for each other, and in consideration of the mutual promises herein expressed, the sufficiency of which is hereby acknowledged, _____ and _____ agree as follows:

ARTICLE I: NAMES

_____ and _____ affirm their individuality and equality in this relationship. The parties reject the concept of ownership implied in the adoption by the woman of the man's name, and they choose to define themselves as husband and wife in the following manner.

The parties agree to retain and use the given family names of each party. The parties will employ the titles of address Mr. and

Ms. and will henceforth be known as partners in this relationship.
It is further agreed that any children born to (them) shall bear (his) family name.

ARTICLE II: RELATIONSHIP WITH OTHERS

_____ and _____ believe that their partnership will be enriched to the extent that their individual needs can be met by relationships with others, and enhanced by the individual growth and experience resulting from such relationships, rather than from total dependence upon each other. The parties are individuals with their own identities, families, interests, histories, and careers. They do not view themselves as an inseparable couple who do not exist apart from each other.

Therefore, the parties agree to allow each other as much time with their friends and in pursuit of their individual interests as they spend with each other. They also agree that invitations extended to one party will not automatically be assumed to include the other.

Further, the parties acknowledge their insecurities about sexual relations beyond the partnership and, therefore, the parties agree to maintain sexual fidelity to each other.

ARTICLE III: CHILDREN

_____ and _____ presently intend to have two children. It is their intention, however, that these children shall be the result of mutual decision, not chance. Therefore, the decision to have each child shall be mutual and deliberate. The parties further agree that the responsibility for birth control shall be shared between them. However, up until the birth of their second child, the primary responsibility for birth control shall rest upon (wife). After the birth of their second child it is mutually agreed that the primary responsibility shall be (husband's). It is the intent of _____ and _____ that upon (husband's) taking primary responsibility for birth control, he may meet that responsibility by vasectomy or other suitable means.

_____ and _____ reject the concept that the primary responsibility for raising children rests with the woman. They believe that such restriction would deprive them of experiences and opportunities both as individuals and as parents and would be detrimental to the growth and development of their children. Therefore, the parties agree that child rearing shall be a mutual privilege and responsibility. In allocating time and duties the parties shall take into account: the demands of their respective careers; their needs as individuals to establish, maintain, and cultivate social and business contacts outside the partnership; their individual skills and desires; and the best interests of their children.

ARTICLE IV: CAREERS AND DOMICILE

_____ and _____ value the importance and integrity of their respective careers and acknowledge the demands that their jobs place on them as individuals and on their partnership. Commitment to their careers will sometimes place stress on the relationship. It has been the experience of the parties that insofar as their careers contribute to individual self-fulfillment, the careers strengthen the partnership.

The parties agree that, should a career opportunity arise for one of the parties in another city at any future time, the decision to move shall be mutual and based upon the following factors:

(a) the overall advantage gained by one of the parties in pursuing the new career opportunity shall be weighed against the disadvantages, economic and otherwise, incurred by the other;

(b) the amount of income from the new job shall not be controlling;

(c) short-term separations as a result of such moves may be necessary;

(d) the personal preference of both parties as to, and inherent advantages and disadvantages of, climate, and location of the new job opportunity.

(Husband) waives whatever right he may have to solely determine the legal domicile of the parties.

ARTICLE V: CARE AND USE OF LIVING SPACE

_____ and _____ recognize the need for autonomy and equality within the home in terms of the use of available space and allocation of household tasks. The parties reject the concept that the responsibility for housework rests with the woman in a marriage relationship while the duties of home maintenance and repair rest with the man.

Therefore, the parties agree to share equally in the performance of all household tasks, taking into consideration individual schedules and preferences.

The parties agree that decisions about the use of living space in the home shall be mutually made, regardless of the parties' relative financial interests in the ownership or rental of the home. Each party shall have an individual area within the home in an equal amount, insofar as space is available.

ARTICLE VI: PROPERTY, DEBTS, LIVING EXPENSES

_____ and _____ intend that the shared responsibility and mutual respect sought in their partnership shall be reflected in the ownership of existing and all future-acquired property, in the characterization and control of income, and in the responsibility for living expenses.

Therefore, the parties agree that this Article of their marriage contract, in lieu of the property laws of this state, shall govern their interests and obligations in all property acquired during their marriage as follows:

A. *Property.*

The parties have made full disclosure to each other of all properties and assets presently owned by each of them, and of the income derived therefrom and from all other sources, and agree that all such property is specifically described in Exhibit A which is incorporated by reference and made a part of this contract.

The parties agree that the wages, salaries, and other income derived by one of the parties shall be separate property of such party to the extent it exceeds the financial responsibilities to the partnership of the individual party. This income shall be subject to the individual control and/or obligation of such party. Such income may be maintained in a separate bank account in the sole name of such party.

Ownership of all future-acquired property, tangible and intangible, will be determined in accordance with the respective contributions of each party, regardless of the proportionate use of such property by the parties. Annually, or sooner if required, the parties agree to amend Exhibit A of this contract to include future-acquired property and any changes in the ownership of property presently described in Exhibit A. The parties may, by mutual agreement, determine their respective interests in an item of property on a basis other than financial contribution, but such agreement shall not be effective until reduced to writing in Exhibit A to this contract. Gifts, bequests or devises made to one of the parties will become the joint property of both parties. Gifts made to both of the parties will also be considered jointly owned.

B. *Debts.*

_____ and _____ are aware of the strain that financial pressures can exert on their partnership. The parties have made full disclosure to each other of all individual debts and financial obligations. These debts and financial obligations are set forth in Exhibit B. The parties agree that they shall be jointly and severally liable for the past and present debts of each other.

The parties agree further that all future expenditures over the sum of One Hundred Dollars ($100.00) shall be mutually agreed upon. Expenditures made pursuant to such agreement shall be the financial responsibility of both parties. The parties agree to share this responsibility in proportion to their individual income.

Expenditures of more than One Hundred Dollars ($100.00) made without the consent of the other party, except in cases of emergency expenditures made in good faith, shall be the sole responsibility of the party making the expenditure and shall be satisfied out of his or her individual income after payment of joint obligations of the partnership.

C. *Living and Other Expenses.*

The parties agree to share responsibility for the normal expenses incurred in daily living in proportion to their respective incomes. These expenses include, but shall not be limited to: (1) mortgage payment or rent; (2) utilities; (3) home maintenance; (4) food; (5) shared entertainment; (6) medical expenses; (7) clothing; and (8) transportation.

The parties recognize that in the absence of income by one party due to unavoidable circumstances such as extended illness or unemployment all debts and expenses of the partnership may become the sole responsibility of the employed party. The parties agree that where one or both parties will be voluntarily without income for an extended period of time, the parties will mutually negotiate such periods.

(Wife) hereby waives whatever right she may have to rely upon (husband) to provide the sole economic support for the family unit.

ARTICLE VII: EVALUATION OF PARTNERSHIP

______ and ______ recognize the importance of change in their relationship and intend that this contract shall be a living document and a focus for periodic evaluations of the partnership.

The parties agree that either party can initiate a review of any article of the contract at any time for amendment to reflect changes in the relationship. The parties agree to honor such requests for review with negotiations and discussions at a mutually convenient time.

The parties agree that, in any event, there shall be an annual review of the provisions of the contract, including Exhibit A, on or about the anniversary date of the execution of the contract.

The parties agree that, in the case of unresolved conflicts between them over any provisions of this contract, they will seek mediation, professional or otherwise, by a third party.

ARTICLE VIII: TERMINATION OF CONTRACT

______ and ______ may by mutual consent terminate this contract at any time.

Furthermore, the parties agree that behavior by either party over a long period of time which indicates substantial noncompliance with the terms and provisions of this contract may be the basis of termination of this contract. Such conduct shall constitute "gross neglect of duty and extreme cruelty" according to the divorce laws of this state.

The parties further agree that in the event of termination of this contract and divorce of the parties, the provisions of this article and article VI of this contract, as amended, shall serve as the final property settlement agreement between the parties. In such event, this contract is intended to effect a complete settlement of any and all claims that either party may have against the other arising from their partnership, and a complete settlement of their respective rights as to alimony, property rights, and all other rights of property otherwise arising out of their partnership.

ARTICLE IX: SAVINGS CLAUSE

The parties intend that should any article of this contract be found to violate public policy, that the remainder of this contract shall still be binding upon them.

ARTICLE X: DECISION MAKING

_____ and _____ share a commitment to a process of negotiations and compromise which will strengthen their equality in the partnership. Decisions will be made with respect for individual needs. The parties hope to maintain such mutual decision-making so that the daily decisions affecting their lives will not become a struggle between the parties for power, authority, and dominance. The parties agree that such a process, while sometimes time-consuming and fatiguing, is a good investment in the future of their relationship and their continued esteem for each other.

Now, therefore, _____ and _____ make the following declarations:

1. They are responsible adults.

2. They freely adopt the spirit and the material terms of this marriage contract.

3. The marriage contract hereby manifests their intent to define the rights and obligations of their marriage relationship as distinct from those rights and obligations defined by the laws of the state and affirms their right to do so.

4. They intend to be legally bound by this marriage contract and to uphold its articles before any court of law in the land.

IN WITNESS WHEREOF . . . .

Financial and Legal Checklist

1. ***State marriage laws.*** (See Appendix.) Find out how to get married in your state. Know the laws concerning marriage and divorce.

2. ***Your names.*** If you are changing your name, be sure your new name appears on the following:
   a. Driver's license
   b. Car registration
   c. Credit cards
   d. Social security
   e. Bank accounts
   f. Insurance policies
   g. Employment records
   h. Pension plans
   i. Passport
   j. Stocks, bonds, property titles
   k. Leases

3. ***Company insurance benefits.*** If both of you work in companies that provide group health insurance, sign up separately, insuring each other. Here's why: most policies will coordinate benefits so that up to 100 percent of the allowable expenses incurred during the year can be paid jointly by the plans.

4. ***Insurance on your own.*** If neither of you has corporate group health insurance, try to get in a group plan through a union or professional association. Take out separate policies on life insurance, if necessary.

5. ***Disability benefits.*** Each of you should have disability coverage, especially if you depend on two incomes.

6. ***Pensions.*** Get individual pensions. If the company provides one with optional investment, go to it. If you're on your own, investigate an Individual Retirement Account or a Keogh Plan.

7. ***Beneficiaries.*** Change beneficiary names on insurance and other benefit plans.

8. ***Wills.*** Consult a lawyer. A simple will costs about fifty dollars; more complicated ones might include naming an executor. Your lawyer will advise you best.

9. ***Credit and credit cards.*** Keep or establish good credit ratings as individuals. You can double up on some cards, especially if the annual fee is high. But it's best to be separate.

10. ***Consult a tax accountant.*** Prepare early for your new tax status. Ask about income averaging or other devices that can save you money.

11. ***Nuptial agreements.*** Consult a lawyer to draw up any ownership agreements or marriage contracts you might want.

Appendix

Marriage Information

Source: Compiled by William E. Mariano, Council on Marriage Relations, Inc., 110 E. 42d St., New York, NY 10017 (as of Mar. 15, 1981)

Marriageable age, by states, for both males and females with and without consent of parents or guardians. But in most states, the court has authority to marry young couples below the ordinary age of consent, where due regard for their morals and welfare so requires. In many states, under special circumstances, blood test and waiting period may be waived.

State	With consent		Without consent		Blood test		Wait for license	Wait after license
	Men	Women	Men	Women	Required	Other state accepted*		
Alabama (b)	14	14	18	18	Yes	Yes	none	none
Alaska	16	16	18	18	Yes	No	3 days	none
Arizona	16(i)	16	18	18	Yes	Yes	none	none
Arkansas	17	16(j)	18	18	Yes	No	3 days	none
California	18(i)	18	18	18	Yes (n)	Yes	none	none
Colorado	16	16	18	18	Yes (n)	—	none	none
Connecticut	16	16(l)	18	18	Yes	Yes	4 days	none
Delaware	18	16(o)	18	18	Yes	Yes	none	24 hrs. (c)
District of Columbia	16	16	18	18	Yes	Yes	3 days	none
Florida	18	18	18	18	Yes	Yes	3 days	none
Georgia	16	16	18	18	Yes	Yes	none (k)	none
Hawaii	16	16	18	18	Yes	Yes	none	none
Idaho	16	16	18	18	Yes (n)	Yes	none (k)	none
Illinois (a)	16	16	18	18	Yes (p)	Yes	none	1 day
Indiana	17(o)	17(o)	18	18	Yes (p)	No	72 hrs.	none
Iowa	16(o)	16(o)	18	18	Yes	Yes	3 days	none
Kansas	14	12	18	18	Yes	Yes	3 days	none
Kentucky	—(o)	—(o)	18	18	Yes	No	3 days	none
Louisiana (a)	18(o)	16(j)	18	16	Yes	No	none	72 hrs.
Maine	16(j)	16(j)	18	18	No	No	5 days	none
Maryland	16	16	18	18	none	none	48 hrs.	none
Massachusetts	—(o)	—(o)	18	18	Yes	Yes	3 days	none
Michigan (a)	18	16	18	18	Yes	No	3 days	none
Minnesota	—	16(e)	18	18	none	—	5 days	none

Mississippi (b)	—	—	17	15	Yes	—	3 days	none
Missouri	15	15	18	18	none	Yes	3 days	none
Montana	15	15	18	18	Yes (n)	Yes	none	3 days
Nebraska	17	17	18	18	Yes (n)	Yes	2 days	none
Nevada	16	16	18	18	none	none	none	none
New Hampshire (a)	14(e)	13(e)	18	18	Yes	Yes	5 days	none
New Jersey (a)	—	12	18	18	Yes	Yes	72 hrs.	none
New Mexico	16	16	18	18	Yes	Yes	none	none
New York	16	14	18	18	Yes (p)	No	none	24 hrs.(g)
North Carolina (a)	16	16	18	18	Yes (p)	Yes	none	none
North Dakota (a)	16	16	18	18	Yes	—	none	none
Ohio (a)	18	16	18	18	Yes	Yes	5 days	none
Oklahoma	16	16	18	18	Yes	No	none (f)(h)	none
Oregon	17	17	18	18	Yes	No	3 days	none
Pennsylvania	16	16	18	18	Yes	Yes	3 days	none
Rhode Island (a) (b)	18	16	18	18	Yes (n)	No	none	none
South Carolina	16	14	18	18	none	none	24 hrs.	none
South Dakota	16	16	18	18	Yes	Yes	none	none
Tennessee (b)	16	16	18	18	Yes	Yes	3 days	none
Texas	14	14	18	18	Yes	Yes	none	none
Utah (a)	14	14	18	18	none	Yes	none	none
Vermont (a)	18	16	18	18	Yes	—	none	5 days
Virginia (a)	16	16	18	18	Yes	Yes (m)	none	none
Washington	17	17	18	18	(d)	—	3 days	none
West Virginia	18	16	18	18	Yes	No	3 days	none
Wisconsin	16	16	18	18	Yes	Yes	5 days	none
Wyoming	16	16	19	19	Yes	Yes	none	none
Puerto Rico	18	16	21	21	(f)	none	none	none
Virgin Islands	16	14	18	18	none	none	8 days	none

***Many states have additional special requirements; contact individual state.** (a) Special laws applicable to non-residents. (b) Special laws applicable to those under 21 years; Ala., bond required if male is under 18, female under 18. (c) 24 hours if one or both parties resident of state; 96 hours if both parties are non-residents. (d) None, but both must file affidavit. (e) Parental consent plus court's consent required. (f) None, but a medical certificate is required. (g) Marriage may not be solemnized within 10 days from date of blood test. (h) If either under 18, 72 hrs. (i) Statute provides for obtaining license with parental or court consent with no state minimum age. (j) Under 16, with parental and court consent. (k) If either under 18, wait 3 full days. (l) If under stated age, court consent required. (m) Va. blood test form must be used. (n) Applicant must also supply a certificate of immunity against German measles (rubella). (o) If under 18, parental and/or court consent required. (p) Statement whether person is carrier of sickle-cell anemia may be required.

Index

A

B

E

F

G

H

I

J

K

L

M

N

O

P

U

V

W

ABOUT THE AUTHOR

Jacqueline McCord Leo is the Fashion Editor of *Modern Bride* magazine and a former editor of *Bride's* magazine. She has been a reporter and feature writer for *The Singapore Herald* and the Associated Press, and has written for *The New York Times Magazine, The Chicago Tribune* and the New York *Daily News.* Ms. Leo is a member of the Coty Awards Committee and Fashion Group.